"Giammona and Anderson take readers on a deep, riveting journey into preparing for the perilous world of the end times with *The Military Guide to Armageddon*. This read is a grand slam!"

Dr. Robert Jeffress, senior pastor, First Baptist Church, Dallas, Texas; contributor, Fox News; adjunct professor, Dallas Theological Seminary; host, *Pathway to Victory*

"My emphasis has been and will always be the glory of God. His glory will be to strengthen us to survive the end times. But it is also necessary for us to prepare our life and soul for the end times. What a great spiritual balance to walk in the glory and to have the manual to prepare for the last scene of the last act of the last book of the Bible, Revelation!"

Sid Roth, host, *It's Supernatural!*

"This book is not only the wake-up call needed for all believers, it is also a powerful spiritual preparation manual that unlocks for all of us how we should live in the last days. It is time for the church to wake up, put on the full armor of God and prepare for what's ahead."

Rabbi Jonathan Bernis, Jewish Voice Ministries International; host, *Jewish Voice with Jonathan Bernis*

"Giammona and Anderson have written a must-read for anyone who aspires to be a warrior for God in the end times. Read this book—and learn from the best."

Dr. Thomas Horn, CEO, SkyWatch TV

"While so much of the Christian world today is content to hide its head in the sand and ignore the many clear warnings and exhortations of the Bible concerning the last days, *The Military Guide to Armageddon* is chock full of wisdom that will help the believer navigate the great challenges and opportunities that lie ahead."

Joel Richardson, *New York Times* bestselling author, teacher, filmmaker

"Col. David Giammona and Troy Anderson have written a must-read primer for anyone considering how to strengthen their walk with God in the end times."

U.S. Army Maj. Gen. Robert F. Dees (Ret.), decorated U.S. army general; associate vice president, Military Outreach, and director, Institute for Military Resilience, at Liberty University; campaign chairman for Dr. Ben Carson; author, *Resilience God Style*

"*The Military Guide to Armageddon* is one of the most important books I have read in a long time! This spiritually powerful and biblically balanced book is essential reading for any leader, man or woman who seeks to obey God's call to be an effective spiritual warrior in these last days. This practical book will teach you how to be battle ready, effective and victorious as a spiritual warrior."

Dr. Paul McGuire, bestselling author

"This is a very timely book, because the signs that Jesus instructed us to watch for just prior to His return are coming to pass right in front of our eyes. I strongly encourage everyone to buy this book and to share it with others. This guide will give you a better understanding of how the military chess pieces are moving into place, and it won't be too long before a major conflict erupts. This is a time of wars and rumors of wars, and the authors have worked hard to give us some insight into what is really going on out there."

Michael Snyder, The Most Important News

"Being a special operator in the Special Warfare Command of the U.S. Navy (ret.), I have a vested interest in war and its complexity. Chaplain Colonel Giammona has mastered the contrast of spiritual and physical war and their similarities with stellar clarity. The best book on end-time preparation I've ever read. Stunning."

M. David Roever, D.D., founder, president, CEO, Operation Warrior RECONnect

# THE
# MILITARY
# GUIDE TO
# ARMAGEDDON

## BATTLE-TESTED STRATEGIES TO PREPARE
## YOUR LIFE AND SOUL FOR THE END TIMES

COL. DAVID J. GIAMMONA

 AND

TROY ANDERSON

**Chosen**

*a division of Baker Publishing Group*
Minneapolis, Minnesota

Published by Chosen Books
11400 Hampshire Avenue South
Bloomington, Minnesota 55438
www.chosenbooks.com

Chosen Books is a division of
Baker Publishing Group, Grand Rapids, Michigan

Printed in the United States of America

Library of Congress Cataloging-in-Publication Data
Names: Giammona, David J., author. | Anderson, Troy (Journalist), author.
Title: The military guide to Armageddon: battle-tested strategies to prepare your life and soul for the end times / Col. David J. Giammona and Troy Anderson.
Description: Minneapolis, Minnesota: Chosen Books, a division of Baker Publishing Group, 2021. | Includes bibliographical references.
Identifiers: LCCN 2020038021 | ISBN 9780800761943 (paperback) | ISBN 9780800762261 (casebound) | ISBN 9781493430086 (ebook)
Subjects: LCSH: Spiritual warfare. | End of the world. | Armageddon.
Classification: LCC BV4509.5 .G466 2021 | DDC 236/.9—dc23
LC record available at https://lccn.loc.gov/2020038021

Cover design by Rob Williams, InsideOut Creative Arts, Inc.

The authors are represented by Alive Communications, Inc.

21  22  23  24  25  26  27     7  6  5  4  3  2  1

We dedicate *The Military Guide to Armageddon*
to all who will pick up the challenge and surrender
their lives for the cause of Christ in the last days.

We dedicate this book to all who are weary of business
as usual and long for something richer, deeper
and more inspiring than ever before.

We dedicate this book to the warriors among us
preparing for spiritual battles in the end times.

Finally we dedicate this book to the entire U.S. military
for their professionalism, bravery and dedication to
"support and defend the Constitution of the United States
against all enemies, foreign and domestic."

4
5
6

P5 130 139+140
142 143

# CONTENTS

## PART 3: ADVANCED TACTICS

# FOREWORD

IT HAS BEEN MY PRIVILEGE to live in "Military City, USA" all my life. As a native of San Antonio, Texas, I have been surrounded by some of the greatest citizens, servants and soldiers the world has ever seen. Their willingness to protect and defend our nation has always been an inspiration to me. Their sacrifice and commitment serve as a constant reminder that I have been called to do the same by my Lord and Savior, Jesus Christ. I am to be a citizen of His Kingdom here on this earth. I am to serve Him with all my heart, soul, mind, strength, and to love my neighbor as myself. I am to be a soldier in His army and take a stand in the evil day. We live in an evil day that seeks to destroy all that is good, and the need for change can no longer be ignored.

Bible-believing Christians cannot afford to be spectators in this culture war that is changing every aspect of our lives. We are watching our freedoms and liberties be trampled beneath a relentless agenda to destroy the foundations of truth, rid society of the institutions of faith and crush the influence of the Church. Some have described it as the "post-Christian era," others choose to use more moderate terms, but the fact remains, we are in a supernatural war in this modern world. The Apostle Paul made it clear that we were going to be engaged in a spiritual battle that would only increase in intensity until Jesus Christ returns to earth to establish His Kingdom. The day of decision for this generation has arrived, and the ancient question echoes still, "Who is on the Lord's side?"

This resource is filled not with theories, suggested strategies and general ideas for you to consider but with real battlefield-tested facts, tactics and information that will convert an apathetic churchgoer into a soldier of salt and light. The authors combine decades of battlefield experience and award-winning investigative journalism to demonstrate what God will do with those who are willing to take a stand, face adversity and make history. The world around you is decaying in darkness; now is the time to answer the question, "What are you going to do about it?"

What are you going to do about the chaos in our streets? This book has the answer. How are you going to lead your family, loved ones and friends with confidence in uncertain times? This book will show you the way. How does this epic conflict end, who will win, and what will happen in the world tomorrow? If you'd like to know, then turn the page.

This book points to truths that can change your life forever. The days in which we live require each of us to choose between light and darkness, good and evil, truth and deception, Christ and Anti-Christ—there is no middle ground. Congratulations on taking a step in the right direction. Thank you for answering the call to be a citizen, a servant and a soldier. You are needed now more than ever. I pray as you read and apply the principles contained in this work that you see the hand of God move in your life like never before. The good fight of faith is still worth fighting. May we all stand our post and serve to the last full measure, until He comes!

Matthew Hagee, lead pastor,
Cornerstone Church, San Antonio, Texas

# PREFACE

I AM PERSUADED that things on this planet are about to change drastically, and that we need to prepare for coming earth-shattering events. In fact, I had a life-changing spiritual encounter (which I will describe in chapter 5) that convinced me that God has called us all to go out and wake up the Church and the world to what is about to happen.

We are about to face the most difficult days in the history of mankind. If we are not prepared, we could be swept away by all the propaganda and politics of the world that Satan is using against us. Unless we are ready—awakened from our sleep and prepared to encounter God—we will not be able to engage fully in the ministry and spiritual warfare God has for us.

The Church in her current state is not ready for the end times or the return of Jesus Christ. We have been paralyzed with fear of what human beings may do to us. But if we are not prepared, we are going to falter or, worse, reject our faith and succumb to the world system and the worship of the Antichrist.

Whether you know it or not, we are at war. The forces of light and darkness are lined up in battle array. You are either on one side or the other; there is no neutral ground.

I learned this in a profound way during 32 years of military service, including tours of combat and other duties in Iraq, Afghanistan, Saudi Arabia and Honduras. I have witnessed war firsthand and can tell you this: Most young soldiers came back from combat very different from when they went in. Many young soldiers (and older ones too, even chaplains) lose their faith in a God they believed would protect them and their buddies from harm.

I am not saying God does not protect, care for and love us—just not in a way most of our troops expected or had previously experienced. They were not prepared for what they encountered. When you are young, idealistic and impressionable, you have an immature worldview. After these soldiers witnessed the true horrors of war—the inhumanity, bloodshed, anxiety, stress and fog of war—they would never be the same.

I have dealt with many of them and their families. Even chaplains returning with the 101st Airborne Division from Operation Iraqi Freedom (OIF) were in shambles on returning home. One chaplain, when I asked him how he was doing, broke into uncontrollable tears from remembering picking up body parts after seventeen of his own soldiers died in a midair Black Hawk helicopter collision.

I include myself in that number. I had all the symptoms of post-traumatic stress disorder. So did my son, who was deployed with a Long-Range Surveillance detachment in OIF. Some things will never leave me, and maybe I don't want them to. I still love God and serve Him, but my worldview has changed because of what I experienced.

Given what I went through, I believe God has called us to prepare people for what is surely to come and help Jesus' followers become end-times warriors for God. Whether or not you believe that the Church will go through the Tribulation (a seven-year period of the greatest trouble, war, persecution and devastation the world has ever witnessed), many believers are not prepared.

Our hope is that this book will open the eyes of your heart. We don't want any of us to be unprepared. Get ready.

# ACKNOWLEDGMENTS

IT TAKES ONLY ONE WORD to explain how this book came into being: God. God set us on a journey to prepare the Church and warn the world of the end-times events coming to planet earth and the coming of the Messiah, Jesus Christ. In addition to the Lord, we want to thank the following people who have been on this astonishing journey with us.

I (David) dedicate this book to Esther, a warrior in her own right, my incredible wife. She has been with me on an astounding forty-plus-year journey around the world to some of the most far-flung and exotic places on the planet. And, of course, to my wonderful and longsuffering kids: Micah, Catarina and Melissa, along with their spouses: Andrea, Andrew and Luis, in addition to my four grandchildren, who are all amazing.

I (Troy) dedicate this book to my beautiful, wise and pure-hearted wife, Irene, whose prayers, enthusiasm and steadfast belief that the Lord has plans for *The Military Guide to Armageddon* far greater than any of us can imagine have been a source of great encouragement for those involved in this incredible project. I also dedicate this book to our charming and delightful daughters, Marlee and Ashley.

David:

There are many along with us on this journey who need thanks. To my best friend of more than 45 years, mentor, pastor and confidant, Coco Perez. He led me to Christ! To Pastor Glen Cole, now in heaven with Christ, who was an enormous influence on me in so many ways.

To my many chaplain friends, peers, bosses and associates. These include my good friend, mentor and leader, and former military chaplain endorser for the Assemblies of God, Scott McChrystal. To the current great Assembly of God military chaplain endorser, Jim Denley. To Manny Cordero, the senior endorser and leader of all Assemblies of God chaplains. To Pete Brzezinski, Mike Dugal, Rod Mills, Terry Austin, Rod Mills, Bob Marsi and Layden Colby, my fellow chaplains and friends.

To my great staff at Installation Command Headquarters, San Antonio; to the greatest and best sergeant major you could ever ask for, Pam Wilson; and to the hardworking Mike Swingler, my deputy and friend.

To my Army commanders and chaplain bosses, who were the best. My last commander was Lieutenant General Ken Dahl and his deputy, the inimitable Major General Warren Patterson, both incredible men and officers. My boss at the Pentagon is the former chief of chaplains, Doug Carver, a great man of God. My other colonel chaplain bosses at the Pentagon were also incredible: Richard Pace, Dave Smartt and Alan Buckner. I want to make special mention of the Chief of Staff for the Chief of Chaplains, Lamar Griffin, who passed away too soon from this life; and to my good friend over the years and current Army Chief of Chaplains, Major General Tom Solhjem.

To the talented Dr. Tim Hager, vice president and dean of the Assemblies of God Theological Seminary. To retired

Major General Bob Dees for the time he took to be interviewed for the book.

We would also like to thank others who graciously took time to do interviews for the book, including Rabbi Jonathan Bernis, Sid Roth, Joel Richardson, Dr. Robert Jeffress, John Ramirez, Dr. Robert Mawire, Lieutenant General Ken Dahl, Colonel Pete Brzezinski, and Lieutenant Colonel Scott Koeman.

In addition, we would like to thank everyone who agreed to endorse the book, including Joel Richardson, Major General Bob Dees, Sid Roth, Rabbi Jonathan Bernis, Dr. Robert Jeffress, Dave Roever, Dr. Thomas R. Horn, Paul McGuire and Michael Snyder.

Special thanks to Pastor Matt Hagee, who wrote the foreword.

Troy:

I would like to thank our Bible study group in Irvine, California, led by David and Esther, who prayed for the Lord's guidance and blessings over this project. I would further like to thank our 45-member Film Prayer Warriors team who prayed for a spiritual covering over *The Military Guide to Armageddon*. I would also like to thank Pastor Jerry Moses, assistant to the president at *Movieguide*, for his Holy Spirit–inspired wisdom, prayers and belief in this project, along with *Movieguide* founder Dr. Ted Baehr, who graciously invited me to attend *Movieguide*'s "How to Succeed in Hollywood (Without Losing Your Soul)" screenwriting class.

Further I would like to thank our team at *GODSPEED* magazine, including publisher Jeremy Lamont, editor-in-chief David Aikman, chief operations officer Jim Weiss, vice president of production Jake Gleim, director of ministry support Rebecca Lamont, and social relations manager Deborah Flook, for their overwhelming support of this project and dedicating the July 2020 "Remnant" issue largely to *The Military Guide to Armageddon,* as well as the Lord's calling on Todd Smith, senior pastor at Christ Fellowship Church in Dawsonville, Georgia, and leader of the North Georgia Revival spreading across the nation, to "build Me an army I can use" in the last days.

We would also like to thank our awesome literary agent, Bryan Norman, president of Alive Literary Agency, for his belief in this project. "Exciting stuff," Norman told us as we were writing the book. "Really pumped about this book."

Also I would like to thank Paul McGuire, co-author of our bestsellers *The Babylon Code* and *Trumpocalypse,* who gave us his blessing for this project, mentored me for many years, and imparted the prophetic wisdom he gained over a lifetime of studying and living the Word of God—setting an example of biblical courage for us all during these perilous times.

Finally we would like to thank our incredible team at Chosen Books, including marketing manager Deirdre Thompson, associate marketing manager Stephanie Smith, marketing and publicity assistant Mycah McKeown, copywriter Rachael Wing, and our amazing editor, Jane Campbell, editorial director of Chosen, who decided to personally edit *The Military Guide to Armageddon.* We would like to thank her for her enthusiasm for the book and confidence that the Lord plans to use this "magnificent and marvelous work to prepare readers for the battle ahead."

PART 1

# BATTLE
# READY!

# 1
# THE MAKING OF A WARRIOR

If you know the enemy and know yourself, you need not fear the results of a hundred battles.

—Sun Tzu, Chinese general, philosopher and military strategist

IT WAS AN ORDINARY, cold Saturday afternoon in January in San Antonio, Texas. My wife and I were driving to Walmart when our youngest daughter, who was living in Honolulu, Hawaii, called from her work as a lifeguard at a hotel on Waikiki Beach. Esther and I could tell that something was terribly wrong.

Melissa's voice trembled as she explained that her fiancé had just called to inform her that a ballistic missile from North Korea had been launched and was on its way toward Hawaii. In fact, at 8:07 A.M. local time, Hawaiian citizens had received an emergency alert on their smartphones that read: BALLISTIC MISSILE THREAT INBOUND TO HAWAII. SEEK IMMEDIATE SHELTER. THIS IS NOT A DRILL.[1]

I pulled off the road into the nearest parking lot. Melissa cried out, "Dad, what do I do?" Immediately I went into Army mode. I told her to remain calm, get to the nearest shelter, and text or call us back from there.

Esther continued to talk with her while I pulled out my Army phone and started scanning for emergency alerts. At the same time my mind and body were in full adrenaline alert. It was as if I had just drunk four cups of Italian espresso.

Multiple thoughts flooded me. Could that madman in North Korea have pulled off a first strike on the United States? Where were our anti-missile defenses? Why hadn't Army headquarters (HQ) alerted me? Were we headed into World War III and all-out nuclear war?

Before those questions were answered, I received a much-needed text from Melissa's fiancé stating that this was a false alarm. One of the workers at the Hawaii Emergency Management Agency (HEMA) had pushed the wrong button, unleashing panic throughout the Hawaiian Islands and the American mainland.

That one mistake in January 2018 sent shock waves around the islands and the world. One additional mistake on either side could have spelled disaster for the planet. With more than three decades in the Army, I had thought I was prepared for everything, but not this. Sure, I was relieved along with Esther and Melissa, but it took several hours to get back to normal. Afterward I could not help but relive what had happened to me some 27 years prior, right after Operation Desert Storm.

Our Patriot Missile Battalion (1–43 ADA) had been sent to Saudi Arabia to protect the oilfields and infrastructure from a still-dangerous Saddam Hussein. Our Bravo Company battery commander told me to get to the concrete underground shelter because radar had detected a Scud missile launch headed for our position. I rushed to the bunker to discover a crowded room full of anxious soldiers awaiting their fate. Thank God it turned out to be a false alarm.

Nevertheless, whether it takes place in Hawaii or the Middle East, conflict and war throughout the history of mankind are inevitable.

## War and Peace

War. We see it in the news constantly.

Over the past 3,400 years, mankind has experienced only 268 years of peace—just eight percent of recorded history. Historians are unsure of the actual number of people killed in war, but some estimate it is up to one billion. War is an integral part of who we are.[2]

History has seen many kinds of war: territorial, regional, national, worldwide, civil, economic and religious. There are many types of modern warfare—conventional, unconventional, nuclear/biological/chemical, and cyber. But another type of conflict has been going on since before the Fall of man in the book of Genesis: the battle in the heavens between the forces of heaven and hell, and the battle that rages within us.

This unseen war is played out every day in our world: the battle of the sexes, intense political conflicts, clashes of worldview, the rise of Islam, religious apostasy, divorce, abortion, addiction, pornography and the overall decay of the human condition.

And each of us, like Adam and Eve, has a choice to make every morning when we get up: whether to choose what God has for us or to choose what we selfishly desire: materialistic things, worldly acclaim, appeasing our fleshly appetites.

Physical battles take place every day on this planet, but the unseen conflict is what is really at the heart of what we are seeing happen in the world. Our nations have been in moral decline for decades. We can stand by and let them sink into oblivion or we can do something about it. We can throw up our hands and give up in the face of our postmodern age, or we can arm ourselves for battle.

In either case, war of the greatest magnitude is here. Are you ready?

## The Bible's Greatest Warrior

Throughout this book we will look at the life of King David, the Bible's greatest warrior, and other biblical heroes, in order to learn how they prepared for and engaged in battle. We will also look at ways to emulate them and find the hidden biblical truths that can unlock God's supernatural power in your life.

As you read the Bible, you get the picture that conflict is part of life. The Bible describes more than ninety battles, and David was in about sixty of them. We can learn a great deal by studying these conflicts. And as you read this book, you will find out what it takes to become a warrior of God in the last days; how to prepare yourself and those around you for coming catastrophic events; and what practical exercises are most effective in transforming you into a battle-ready believer.

While obtaining a Master of Strategic Studies at the U.S. Army War College in Carlisle, Pennsylvania, I often studied the life of David and the battles he was involved in. Studying the biblical figure God called a "man after his own heart" (1 Samuel 13:14) helped prepare me for my last assignment at the Installation Management Command (IMCOM) at Fort Sam Houston in San Antonio, Texas.

At IMCOM, I was responsible for overseeing religious support at all 75 Army installations worldwide, along with more than one thousand chaplains and several thousand volunteers worldwide. I was the strategic advisor to a three-star commanding general and chief executor to the chief of chaplains. The generals and other high-ranking officials I worked under also studied the life of David, since there is much to learn from the biblical account of one of the greatest warrior-kings of all time.

## Signs of Jesus' Return

A Barna Group poll several years ago found 41 percent of American adults, 54 percent of Protestants, and 77 percent of evangelical Christians believe the world is now living in the "biblical end times."[3] And as the COVID-19 coronavirus was spreading around the world in late 2019 and 2020, a LifeWay Research poll found that nine in ten pastors saw at least some current events matching those that Jesus said would occur shortly before His return to earth.[4] Many high-ranking military officials, along with faith leaders and Bible scholars interviewed for this book, agree that the world is on the precipice of major events that will change life dramatically on this planet.

As the world edges closer to what Matthew 24:3 describes as "the end of the age," we see signs everywhere that point to the return of Jesus Christ. The world is at a precarious point with many Scripture prophecies either fulfilled or in various stages of fulfillment.

One of the primary developments that tell us we are living in the end times is the rebirth of Israel in 1948. Isaiah 66:8 tells us:

> "Who has ever heard of such things? Who has ever seen things like this? Can a country be born in a day or a nation

be brought forth in a moment? Yet no sooner is Zion in labor than she gives birth to her children."

Israel was literally born in a day with the Balfour Declaration, a statement of British support for "the establishment in Palestine of a national home for the Jewish people." The declaration was made in a letter from British Foreign Secretary Arthur James Balfour to Lionel Walter Rothschild, a leader of British Jewry, on November 2, 1917.[5]

Then, several decades later, on May 14, 1948, following a United Nations plan to partition Palestine into Jewish and Arab sections, Jewish Agency Chairman David Ben-Gurion proclaimed the State of Israel, establishing the first Jewish state in two millennia. Ben-Gurion went on to become Israel's first premier.[6]

Israel and the surrounding Middle Eastern countries have since taken center stage in world events. The last days are centered on the Middle East. Israel lies at the very heart of biblical prophecy, and it is where Christ will return to set up His eternal Kingdom. He will reign from Jerusalem. Consider these Scriptures:

> The Lord will rule over them in Mount Zion from that day and forever. As for you, watchtower of the flock, stronghold of Daughter Zion, the former dominion will be restored to you; kingship will come to Daughter Jerusalem.
>
> Micah 4:7–8

> At that time they will call Jerusalem The Throne of the Lord, and all nations will gather in Jerusalem to honor the name of the Lord. No longer will they follow the stubbornness of their evil hearts.
>
> Jeremiah 3:17

Other last days events include the recapture of Jerusalem in the Six-Day War in 1967 (see Luke 21:24); the realignment of the Middle East with Iran and Turkey as major military powers; plans to build the futuristic city of Neom in Saudi Arabia (we believe it could be what Revelation 17–18 describes as "Babylon the Great," the headquarters of the Antichrist); and plans to build the Third Temple in Jerusalem (Matthew 24:15).

We are on the edge of some extraordinary events, including the rise of the Antichrist and the fulfillment of many other Bible prophecies. Nearly one-third of Scripture is predictive in nature, and the world has watched many of these prophecies unfold in recent decades. When you look at the world today, you can see that Jesus' predictions and Satan's plans are coming to pass.

The devil is doing everything he can to Balkanize and segregate the world to break us up into increasingly hostile groups. Thus we fail to recognize that we are all created in the image of God and that there is only one enemy, according to Scripture—the adversary, Satan himself. He has convinced most of us that we are each other's enemies.

Today there is profound division among mankind: "Nation will rise against nation, and kingdom against kingdom" (Matthew 24:7). Meanwhile, natural and manmade disasters are demonstrably increasing in both frequency and intensity. Scientific studies reveal that earthquakes, or natural disasters resulting in significant destruction of property or loss of life, are also increasing in number and intensity.[7]

Further, some of today's technological advances—weapons of mass destruction, electronic banking, microchip implants, the internet, artificial intelligence, and the surveillance state—mirror events the apostle John described in the book of Revelation.

Consider Revelation 9:2–6:

> When he opened the Abyss, smoke rose from it like the smoke from a gigantic furnace. The sun and sky were darkened by the smoke from the Abyss. And out of the smoke locusts came down on the earth and were given power like that of scorpions of the earth. They were told not to harm the grass of the earth or any plant or tree, but only those people who did not have the seal of God on their foreheads. They were not allowed to kill them but only to torture them for five months. And the agony they suffered was like that of the sting of a scorpion when it strikes. During those days people will seek death but will not find it; they will long to die, but death will elude them.

In the military, the advent of weaponized autonomous drones is already here. These sophisticated unmanned drones can swarm like locusts and are encoded with "algorithms for countless human-defined courses of action to meet emerging challenges." Perdix autonomous microdrones have already been dropped from an F-18 fighter jet in a successful test.[8] Such drones can be weaponized and, in the future, potentially bring down the population of an entire city without destroying the buildings or leaving residual radiation as nuclear weapons would. The prospects of these autonomous technologies—whether flying drones, underwater vehicles or other lethal weapon systems—are the future of war.

I was given an opportunity to witness the General Atomics MQ-1C Gray Eagle drone at a U.S. Army installation. It is an upgrade of the MQ-1 Predator. One of its operators told me that this drone can be put into autonomous mode in which it can take off, perform the mission and return—all on its own.

Technologically advanced warfare is looming on many fronts. Iran seeks to dominate the Middle East, including Israel. Turkey also wants to be the regional power and new Islamic caliphate. China and Russia seek to be regional and world powers and peers with the United States.

Former U.S. Secretary of State Henry Kissinger warned a crowd in Beijing in 2019 that China and the United States are in the "foothills of a Cold War"—adding that the trade war between the two nations, if unchecked, could escalate into a global armed conflict.[9]

These are just a few of the signs that Jesus told His disciples in Matthew 24 that would indicate that His return is approaching. As polls show, most evangelical Christians have looked at events and concluded that what Jesus and the prophets predicted thousands of years ago is coming to pass.

## Virus Outbreak

As Troy and I were finishing this book, the COVID-19 pandemic erupted, gripping the world with panic and trepidation. In the middle of it, my wife and I traveled to Israel and then went to Petra, a historical and archaeological city in southern Jordan where, according to tradition, Moses struck a rock and water gushed out. Prophets like Daniel and Isaiah, and even Jesus Himself, spoke about the monumental structures at Petra in connection with end-times prophecies. You probably glimpsed Petra in movies like *Indiana Jones and the Last Crusade* and *The Mummy Returns*.

While returning from Petra to Jerusalem with a tour group of forty people and six personnel, things became tense at the first checkpoint in Jordan. The first person to greet Esther and me was a Jordanian dressed in surgical garb with a mask to take our temperatures. It was surreal. After crossing the

Jordanian border with a myriad of questions, we arrived at Israel border security, where we were asked many questions about the sites we had visited.

We made it out of that area, thinking we were home free, and headed toward Jerusalem where the Israeli Defense Forces had another checkpoint set up. Our driver asked us to pray that they would not stop us, although they had stopped every tour bus coming into the city before us. We prayed and they waved us through—and our bus erupted in jubilation!

In the year prior to going to Israel, while in prayer and meditation, I asked the Lord about the timing of the release of this book, which is designed to prepare you for living in the end times. He told me that 2020 would be a year of signs that the end times are upon us. He also told me that by the time the book is released, people will need the book due to all the things happening on the earth.

Well, it does not take a rocket scientist—or a prophet of the Lord—to figure out that we are in the midst of end-times events. These have already happened at the time of our writing: not only the coronavirus epidemic, but locusts invading East Africa and the Middle East, massive fires in Australia and around the world, murder hornets invading America, economic woes, fear, and a host of other phenomena.

Here is our take on the coronavirus outbreak. After it subsides, there will be a lull, until the next wave hits the earth. This cycle will repeat with more intense peaks and fewer times of calm, just like a pregnancy—until the return of Christ.

Jesus told us in Matthew 24:6–8 (WEB) that there would be plagues (or virus outbreaks) in the end times:

> "You will hear of wars and rumors of wars. See that you aren't troubled, for all this must happen, but the end is not

yet. For nation will rise against nation, and kingdom against kingdom; and there will be famines, plagues, and earthquakes in various places. But all these things are the beginning of birth pains."

Author and political commentator Joel C. Rosenberg points out that the Bible uses ancient Hebrew and Greek words for *pestilence* and *plagues* at least 127 times. He writes:

Throughout the Bible, we see repeated examples of God using diseases to accomplish His divine and sovereign purposes. There are also Biblical prophecies that warn us that God intends to use terrible, infectious diseases to accomplish His divine and sovereign purposes in the future. . . . In the Gospels, the Lord Jesus Christ warns His disciples that "pestilences" will be one of the signs of the "last days" of human history, a time of shaking the world to wake up and realize that Christ's return to judge and reign over the earth is increasingly imminent.[10]

## The Church Is Not Ready

This book is a wake-up call to prepare for the last of the last days. We don't know the day of the coming of the Lord. But we need to be ready and prepared for that day by being the warriors God intended us to be—not by hiding or fretting, but by preparing for the coming King.

We don't know what hardships we will face, but let's be ready. In becoming a warrior ready for the rigors of battle, there are some clear steps to take. We will look at these action items closely throughout this book.

Powerful forces are lined up for battle. We see it every day in the news. The battle rages for supremacy in the political, social, environmental, religious and governmental spheres. Just when you think you have heard and seen it all, an even deadlier and more vicious attack overshadows the rest.

We are in a battle for our souls. Our eternal destinies, as well as those of billions of people worldwide, hang in the balance. Every day we have choices to make. You are on either one side or the other. If you are not aware of this battle, then you are already one of its victims and a POW (prisoner of war).

Yes, spiritual battle is uncomfortable. It is not politically correct and can be downright scary. We would rather talk about warm feelings, love and the weather. But while many preachers say we are in the age of moral relativism and postmodernism that cannot be reversed, we must not lay down our weapons and give up.

## Benefits of This Book

This book is about how best to prepare yourself and your family for the unseen war, the battle of the ages, that you have already entered. As I noted near the beginning of this chapter, this war began before the Fall of humanity and will continue until Christ returns on His white horse with the armies of heaven during the last great battle—the Battle of Armageddon. The times we live in and the vast array of signs, converging as never before in history, are pointing us to the very time of the end and the great distress coming upon the earth.

*The Military Guide to Armageddon* will help you get ready through what is known in the Army as the process of "the making of a warrior." As a beneficiary of the military and spiritual wisdom condensed in this book, you will:

1. Learn how to apply important military disciplines and strategies to energize an amazing spiritual life.
2. Undergo a personal "great awakening" to the fact that the end times are upon us.
3. Become a dynamic, energized and fully armored warrior of God.
4. Discover and develop spiritual gifts to be able to walk in the supernatural power, provision and protection of the Holy Spirit in the end times.
5. Find out how to engage the enemy on a new level of spiritual warfare based on biblical and military principles.
6. Experience a reinvigoration and passion for reading and studying the Bible as real-time world events and biblical prophecies intersect.
7. Gain an understanding of historical Christian persecution to help you weather the hostility toward believers during the run-up to the return of Christ to establish His Kingdom on earth.

# 2
# BATTLE READY!

Satan is satisfied with all our religious activity as long as it does not move us to break down those gates to rescue the perishing. Therefore, at the top of my agenda these days has been the question: how can I get myself and the church awake to a wartime mentality? Is there some way to break the spell? Picture a great army asleep with mighty weapons in their limp hands and armor in their tents. Picture them sleeping in the fields all around one of Satan's strongholds. Suddenly, an eyelid blinks, a head lifts and looks around. Then another and another. A strange awakening spreads through the field. Muscles are flexed. Armor fitted. Swords sharpened. Eyes meet with silent excitement. The light in the commander's tent goes on, the generals gather and the strategy for the attack is laid.

—John Piper, *Desiring God*

"Therefore keep watch, because you do not know the day or the hour."

—Matthew 25:13

IT WAS ABOUT 0530 at Camp Victory, a military base camp surrounding Baghdad International Airport in Iraq. I was running near the perimeter wall for my morning physical training. The wall was between twelve and fifteen feet high with guard towers spaced evenly along the wall. I ran almost every morning I was in camp. It was good for me, both physically and mentally.

But something was different on this particular morning in 2005. It was eerily quiet and nobody else was around. Besides that, I felt that somebody or something was watching me. I could not shake it off.

From out of nowhere, our battalion S1 (the personnel administrator) came running toward me, agitated, his face white as a ghost.

"Chaplain," he said, "get out of here! There's a sniper on the minaret on the other side of the wall."

Just then a bullet struck the palm tree right above us, and birds scattered from its branches. About the same time, two U.S. Marine Corps AH-1 Cobra helicopters flew over the wall and lit up that minaret with devastating fire. It was right out of a war movie scene, only I was living it.

Snipers routinely use deception as part of their strategy of taking you out. They want you to think all is well and then they kill you. And that sniper had it out for me. I was an easy target—alone, running the perimeter, no one else around me.

I look back at that episode and wonder what would have happened if our battalion S1 had not warned me, or if God had not protected me. I was not battle ready that morning, and it almost cost me my life. I had thought all was well and, despite my misgivings, took no precautions to check out if anything was different on my run. I had never thought that my life might end in the safety and confidence of being inside the wire.

## Reasons for Becoming Battle Ready

The number-one priority in the U.S. Army is being battle ready. No other priority comes close. None. Readiness means that the Army is prepared to fight any conflict, anytime, anywhere in the world—at a moment's notice. If it were not, it would most certainly lose wars. In fact, there are specified units in the Army called Rapid Deployment Forces (RDFs) that can be "wheels up" (en route by aircraft) within eighteen hours. The soldiers in those units carry smartphones constantly in case of recall.

The Bible tells us that a time is coming on this earth of great distress, persecution, upheaval in the social order, and mass deception. As a result, we must be ready and vigilant.

A friend of mine, retired U.S. Army Lieutenant General Ken Dahl, former commanding general at IMCOM, says that just as soldiers need to be ready to fight and win the nation's wars, today's believers need to be prepared for global upheaval and the return of Christ. "If you're searching for strength," he says, "given what you're going to face, prepare yourself for it, recognizing that this is going to be one of the most difficult, if not the most difficult, thing you've ever faced."[1]

Just as military forces train for specific engagements with the enemy, believers need to do the same. Before we look at what it takes to be battle ready in the end times, we need to understand why we need to get prepared.

The Bible says that the rise of the Antichrist will come about because of religious, financial and social chaos, prompting humanity to clamor for a savior or messiah. With the advent of modern technologies, along with biblical prophecies that describe our modern world in remarkable detail, we should not be surprised if the Antichrist exploits our technological tools to gain control of humanity.

A BBC article quotes Rossiya 1, Patriarch Kirill, primate of the Russian Orthodox Church, as saying this on Russian state television:

> "The Antichrist is the person who will be at the head of the worldwide web, controlling all of humankind," he said. "Every time you use your gadget, whether you like it or not, whether you turn on your location or not, somebody can find out exactly where you are, exactly what your interests are and exactly what you are scared of."[2]

The National Security Agency tool called "XKeyscore" collects "nearly everything a user does on the internet," and NSA analysts need no prior authorization to search what you have done on the web. The technology sweeps up "emails, social media and browsing history." A database tracks each keystroke. NSA training materials describe it as their "widest-reaching" online intelligence gathering tool ever.[3]

The rise of Adolf Hitler prior to World War II is a prime example of how things might look. Under Hitler, millions of Jewish people, along with others deemed subhuman (*Untermensch*) by Nazi Germany, suffered severe persecution and genocide. The United States Holocaust Memorial Museum, America's official memorial to the Holocaust, estimates the total number of people murdered at seventeen million, including six million Jews and eleven million others.[4]

As horrific as it was, the Holocaust will pale in comparison to the Antichrist's reign of terror, with an astounding array of technologies at the fingertips of the "man of lawlessness" (2 Thessalonians 2:3) to control humanity and terminate anyone who dissents. Today, even before his arrival on the world stage, the persecution and genocide of Christians are worse "than at any time in history," according to a study by a Roman Catholic organization, Aid to the Church in Need.[5]

This study, and another one by Open Doors, found that a record 245 million Christians are experiencing severe persecution worldwide. Many of them are tortured, raped, imprisoned, beheaded, crucified. Others wind up losing their livelihoods, savings and homes due to persecution.[6] So persecution and martyrdom are not just a thing of the past. They are not just happening on the other side of the world. They are spreading all over the globe, and the Bible tells us it is going to get profoundly worse.

One of the reasons we need to become battle ready, then, is not only that we are already experiencing persecution and satanic oppression and attacks on many levels, but that coming end-times events beckon us to go to the next level of readiness.

## The Battle of the Ages

We look around today and think we are fighting a political or social battle. But while it may look like that at first glance, it is much deeper. In truth, sinister warfare is taking place in the unseen world. This book is about how best to prepare yourself for this conflict—the invisible war in which you are already involved. This is the battle of the ages.

The book of Daniel gives us a glimpse into the reality of spiritual warfare:

> Then [the angel] continued, "Do not be afraid, Daniel. Since the first day that you set your mind to gain understanding and to humble yourself before your God, your words were heard, and I have come in response to them. But the prince of the Persian kingdom resisted me twenty-one days. Then

Michael, one of the chief princes, came to help me, because I was detained there with the king of Persia."

Daniel 10:12–13

The angel speaking to Daniel fought with the "king of Persia" (today's Iran) for three weeks. It was only when one of the chief angels, the archangel Michael, came to help him that he broke through enemy lines to get to Daniel. Gabriel had been resisted not by a human being, but by what is referred to by the apostle Paul in Ephesians 6:12 as one of the "spiritual forces of evil in the heavenly realms." The dark lord of Persia is still there today, causing havoc and war in the Middle East.

When Christ returns on His white horse with the armies of heaven, the Bible tells us that Jesus' followers will be part of the last great battle—the Battle of Armageddon. Revelation 19:11–16 describes the scene:

> I saw heaven standing open, and there before me was a white horse, whose rider is called Faithful and True. With justice he judges and wages war. His eyes are like blazing fire, and on his head are many crowns. He has a name written on him that no one knows but he himself. He is dressed in a robe dipped in blood, and his name is the Word of God. The armies of heaven were following him, riding on white horses and dressed in fine linen, white and clean. Coming out of his mouth is a sharp sword with which to strike down the nations. "He will rule them with an iron scepter." He treads the winepress of the fury of the wrath of God Almighty. On his robe and on his thigh he has this name written: KING OF KINGS AND LORD OF LORDS.

According to the book of Revelation, Armageddon (*Har-Megiddo* in Hebrew, or "hill of Megiddo") is the prophesied location of a gathering of armies for the final battle. Armageddon is in the Jezreel Valley, or the valley of Megiddo, in northern Israel. The valley is approximately twenty miles long by fourteen miles wide—or 280 square miles. From about 3000 BC to the early twentieth century, it was a strategic pass on major international military and trade routes and the location of many decisive battles that changed the course of history.

Recently an oil and gas company discovered "an oil bonanza" in the area "with the potential of billions of barrels." The chief geologist said the oil layer is 350 meters thick—ten times larger than the average oil find worldwide. This may explain why this valley will be the center of the final conflict.

But Armageddon is a much broader term symbolizing a worldwide war culminating in the return of Christ.[7] The Battle of Armageddon is the culmination of all battles and wars in human history. It involves the return of our Lord to destroy the Antichrist, the false prophet and the kings of the earth, along with their armies, as described in Revelation 19:19–21:

> Then I saw the beast and the kings of the earth and their armies gathered together to wage war against the rider on the horse and his army. But the beast was captured, and with it the false prophet who had performed the signs on its behalf. With these signs he had deluded those who had received the mark of the beast and worshiped its image. The two of them were thrown alive into the fiery lake of burning sulfur. The rest were killed with the sword coming out of the mouth of the rider on the horse, and all the birds gorged themselves on their flesh.

When our adversary, Satan, tried to usurp God's position and authority in heaven, God cast him out of the divine realm along with one-third of the angels who rebelled with him. (We will talk about this in more detail in the next chapter.) Ever since this revolt, there has been intense, sustained conflict between the forces of heaven and hell.

## Raising Up End-Times Warriors

What the Church needs more than anything today is an army of supernatural, Bible-believing, Holy Spirit–empowered people of God who are ready and willing to turn a generation upside down for Jesus and do mighty exploits, as templated in the New Testament.

The early Church, as described in the book of Acts, did turn the ancient world upside down, and today's end-times warriors of Christ need to reclaim the sound theology and radical zeal of the first-century Christians. The early Church revolutionized the ancient world in one generation. One of the reasons they were able to do this is that they carried with them the urgency of the biblical message about "the great and dreadful day of the LORD" (Joel 2:31).

The same urgency is trumpeted by Isaiah, Joel, Zephaniah and other Old Testament prophets, who said that people must repent because the Day of the Lord was near. Jesus said essentially the same thing: "Repent, for the kingdom of heaven has come near" (Matthew 4:17).

The primary message of the end times is one of urgency— urgency to proclaim the good news, to complete the Great Commission (Jesus' last command to take the Gospel to all the world), to be holy, and to be ready at any moment to stand before the judgment seat of Christ.

The early believers also had a biblical theology of suffering and even martyrdom. This theology is consistent throughout Scripture. Paul wrote, "Everyone who wants to live a godly life in Christ Jesus will be persecuted" (2 Timothy 3:12). And Jesus said: "If the world hates you, keep in mind that it hated me first. . . . Remember what I told you: 'A servant is not greater than his master.' If they persecuted me, they will persecute you also" (John 15:18, 20).

But today most of the modern Church proclaims a gospel of self-betterment. "It's a very self-focused gospel," says a friend we deeply respect, author and filmmaker Joel Richardson, "which has all but lost a proper theology of suffering, a theology of the cross, a theology of martyrdom." He continues:

> The early Church had an urgency and genuine theology of laying their lives down every day. So it's essential to reclaim the message of the end times, because the Scriptures say it's going to be a time of unparalleled tribulation for the saints—both for Israel and for those in Revelation 12 who keep the commandments of Jesus. If this is the final generation that will face this great time of trial, it's essential that we reclaim the theology and life and character of the early Church.[8]

## Where Are the Bonhoeffers?

Just as the world was not prepared for World War II less than a century ago, neither are we prepared for what the Bible warns is on the horizon.

In the twentieth century, the Church in Germany under the rule of Adolf Hitler was not ready for what was about to happen. Believers witnessed the rise of Hitler, who like many other dictators throughout history embodied the "spirit of the antichrist" (1 John 4:3). Sadly, many churches joined him in support of what they mistakenly believed would be a new and better day in Germany—which at the time was in the throes of the Great Depression.

Will the same thing occur again in our time? If we don't prepare now, we are doomed to repeat history. German pastor Dietrich Bonhoeffer was one of the lone voices that stood against the Third Reich—and he paid for it with his life.

Where are the Bonhoeffers of our time? Let them arise and warn the world of the dark agenda gaining support worldwide.

This book is a forewarning to prepare for the most cataclysmic and profound event in human experience—the end of history when everything described in the book of Revelation occurs and Christ returns. Matthew 24:36 tells us that that no one knows "that day or hour," except the Father; but Jesus told us to be ready and watch for signs of His return.

As the world sees what many Bible scholars believe is an unparalleled convergence and acceleration in end-times signs, the Church is not, for the most part, talking about them or addressing what is happening. Few pastors today give sermons on Bible prophecy and the Second Coming of Christ.

The great irony is that, even as polls show that most evangelical Christians believe end-times events are now unfolding, the Church is mostly silent. In the final chapter of the human story, the Bible tells us that Satan will lead "the whole world astray." In Revelation 12:7–9 the apostle John saw the following in a vision:

> Then war broke out in heaven. Michael and his angels fought against the dragon, and the dragon and his angels fought back. But he was not strong enough, and they lost their place in heaven. The great dragon was hurled down— that ancient serpent called the devil, or Satan, who leads

the whole world astray. He was cast down and his angels with him.

As the Day of the Lord (see Joel 2:31 and Acts 2:20) approaches, believers must learn what the Bible has to say about how to stand firm in the last days and not be swept away by the evil tide. Maintaining the status quo will be a critical, if not fatal, mistake. Our intensity in seeking the Kingdom of God and His supernatural favor must increase exponentially if we are to be effective in the last days.

We are good, for the most part, at winning people to Christ, but we do a poor job of transforming new believers into authentic disciples of Jesus. If the Church is to pass through the coming storm, we need to infuse people with the intensity and focus of the first-century believers—making not just converts but radical followers of Jesus. Far too many of us are asleep at the wheel as events predicted in the Bible unfold all around us.

Jesus' Parable of the Ten Virgins in Matthew 25:1–13 has something important to say. In that story five virgins took extra oil for their lamps as they waited for the arrival of the bridegroom, but the other five did not. And when he finally arrived, later than expected, those five who were unprepared found their lamps going out because they did not have enough oil.

My friend U.S. Army Chaplain (Lieutenant Colonel) Scott Koeman, who served with me in the wars of Afghanistan and Iraq, says about this parable:

> They are sleeping, their lamps are burning, but they don't have enough oil—they are not taking Christ and His calling seriously. In the parable the bridegroom says, "Away from me. I don't know you." Those are hard words, but there are

many churches today that don't preach the hard truth. They are preaching the easy, broad path: "It's all about you and your wealth, what blessings you're receiving, and how the Lord wants to bless you." The emphasis is not on preparedness and a relationship with Christ, which are reflected by the five virgins who had enough oil and were ready for the coming of the bridegroom.[9]

The Church must do what the military does in basic training: convert civilians into soldiers. On the first day of basic training, a civilian becomes a soldier. But it takes months of intense military training to transform that individual into a combat-ready soldier who can help propel the military to victory against its enemies.

Some will say, "I am being taken up in the Rapture of the Church; I have nothing to worry about"—referring to when Jesus Christ returns to "rapture" believers, removing them instantaneously and supernaturally from the world. But if you lived in the days before, during and after World War II in Germany, you would not say that. No one can guarantee we will escape the coming distress of the last days.

## An End-Times Model

A battle-ready believer is described in Acts 13:22: "God testified concerning [David]: 'I have found David son of Jesse, a man after my own heart; he will do everything I want him to do.'" A battle-ready believer uses David as his or her template. The Bible's greatest warrior is an incredible example of how to prepare for and engage in battle.

Battle-ready believers are willing to obey and follow hard after God in every area of life. They are team-centered (not me-centered), mission-oriented and Spirit-filled. They are prayer warriors, trained in the weapons of spiritual warfare, gifted and empowered, disciplined and courageous, ready to do battle with the forces of this present darkness.

Let's look at the life of King David through the lens of modern Army tactics so we, too, can learn how to prepare for battle.

David became a warrior by the seemingly insignificant things he did every day: practicing the basics, being disciplined, obeying his father, being faithful in his responsibilities, training as Saul's armor-bearer, and most of all, doing God's will. King David was involved in both physical and spiritual conflict during his life.

As a shepherd, David protected his flock and fought off bears and lions with only a staff or club. He made sure his sheep had food and water and moved them to greener pastures when necessary. He still tended the flock for his father when his brothers went off to battle. Those things taught David discipline, helped him succeed when he fought his first major battle—the one with Goliath—and were instrumental in his journey from shepherd to warrior to king.

Throughout this book we will learn from David how to become a warrior of God in the last days. Imperfect as he was, he was still a man of great military savvy. The principles he used are studied today in many branches of military service.

Primarily, David exhibited great courage when he stood up to Goliath, a vitally important characteristic for soldiers and warriors of God. Although he was a youth, and though the whole army behind him was terrified, he stood up against the giant with confidence. David shouted across the battlefield, "I come against you in the name of the LORD Almighty, the God of the armies of Israel, whom you have defied" (1 Samuel 17:45).

The Church today can learn much from David, who trusted in God and as a result was fearless. He was willing to take on a giant.

Where are the Davids of this generation who will arise and confront the Goliaths of our time because they have confidence in the Lord and are not afraid of losing their own lives? They are not afraid of losing anything because they know that the battle belongs to the Lord.

## Becoming Battle Ready

Readiness is a top priority not only of the Army but also of the entire military. Here is what former Chief of Naval Operations Admiral J. J. Clark said about future military readiness:

> The world is dangerous and unpredictable. Our Navy routinely operates in tough places, and that's as it should be. We work and operate in an atmosphere of risk and we should not shy away from it. We should be credible and we should be ready. We must constantly challenge the assumptions that we face on a daily basis and adapt to an ever-changing world. . . . It is my conviction that tomorrow's world will be more violent than the past.[10]

Given what the military foresees and the Bible tells us the future holds, we need to refocus on being battle ready. To do this we will, in the next chapter, get to know our enemy better.

The Bible tells us that the power of evil will continue to multiply in strength and numbers in the end times. So we must learn to identify the enemy behind the human powers and initiatives. If you cannot identify your enemy, you will lose every time. In the military you learn that you cannot defeat an enemy you do not know or understand. To address this, we need strategies and tactics to implement our plan. As we hear the hoofbeats of the Four Horsemen of the Apocalypse approaching, knowing and understanding our real enemy will be key.

Just as the Army's term *readiness* is the key driver in preparing soldiers for combat, we, too, need to apply military principles to Christian readiness to become battle-ready believers. The bullet points below compare principles of Army readiness and Christian readiness for you to apply to your own life.

## MILITARY READINESS PRINCIPLES

* Readiness is one of the Army's top priorities.
* Soldiers must always be ready to "fight tonight!"
* The Army must prepare its total forces to meet global military demands while remaining postured for unexpected contingencies.
* Readiness training helps soldiers respond to emerging threats to national security; deploy to combat zones; and project national power.
* Readiness efforts also focus on ballistic missile defense, cyber defense, special operations and cooperation with other military agencies and nations to deter or defeat threats.
* Readiness focuses on a unit's personal readiness and readiness to deploy.
* The Army will continue to rebuild, reinvigorate and develop "total force readiness" to meet developing global threats and win wars.

## BELIEVER'S READINESS PRINCIPLES

* The believer's top priority is to be constantly vigilant and ready for the rise of the Antichrist and return of Jesus Christ (see Matthew 24:42).

* We are in constant spiritual warfare with the enemy and must always be ready to "fight tonight!" (see 1 Peter 5:8).

* We must always be ready to go into all the world to preach the good news. The fight is global (see Mark 16:15).

* "Total force effort" for the believer means joining with other believers as the Church makes war against the enemy (see Matthew 18:20).

* Sustainable readiness for believers in the end times means seeking the Lord constantly and being renewed by the transforming of our minds so we will not be deceived (see Romans 12:2).

* We need to be in constant training to meet the demands of a global increase in persecution and stress in the end times (see Hebrews 10:25).

* We need to seek advanced training in spiritual warfare by studying the Word of God, praying and growing under godly leadership (see 2 Timothy 2:15).

## STRATEGIC SPIRITUAL EXERCISES

Here are five practical action steps to help you become battle ready:

1. Take an inventory of where you are spiritually in your relationship to Jesus Christ and your fellow believers.

2. Look at other believers you know. Find one who is a warrior of God and whom you want to emulate.
3. Don't go it alone. Find others who are passionate for God with whom you can connect.
4. Practice the basics. Start small—but start. Talk with God in your everyday life. Make Him the center of your life. Include Him in all the routine activities of your life.
5. Make plans to get away and spend some alone time with God. Make this your special retreat to restart the next phase of your journey with your Creator.

# 3

# KNOWING YOUR ENEMY

For our struggle is not against flesh and blood, but against the rulers, against the authorities, against the powers of this dark world and against the spiritual forces of evil in the heavenly realms.

—Ephesians 6:12

THE U.S. ARMY EMPHASIZES realistic combat training for a reason. I saw this firsthand in the early 1990s at what was then called the Combat Maneuver Training Center (CMTC) in Hohenfels, Germany. (Today it is called the Joint Multinational Readiness Center, or JMRC.)

We trained "force on force," meaning the opposing army used the type of weaponry and tactics that peer countries, such as Russia, would use against U.S. forces in war. In this case it was "armor vs. armor" (tank on tank), consisting of three weeks of nonstop, realistic combat training in some of the most unforgiving terrain and weather in the world. After every battle scenario, there would be an After-Action Review (AAR)—a structured review or "debrief" (debriefing) process, analyzing what happened, why it happened, and what unit leaders and those responsible for training could do better.

After one such training session with one of our sister battalions, the commander (a lieutenant colonel) was being debriefed in the AAR building while we waited outside. Those debriefings could be intense. Suddenly a medical team arrived with a stretcher, disappeared inside and, moments later, emerged carrying the commander toward a waiting ambulance.

Of course, we were all wondering what happened. Later we learned that the commander had frozen up during the debrief and become nonresponsive to questions. He just froze in place, staring off into space. Stress, lack of sleep and the burden of command had proved too much for him. The high operational tempo pointed to a weakness in the command structure.

Perhaps if that commander had understood his limitations, how he reacted under stress, and how lack of sleep and long hours of training affected him, he could have avoided freezing up, and maybe even delegated his authority to other trusted staff. His real enemy was lurking inside himself.

Realistic training reveals who we are and how we will react in combat. No military wants to put leaders of soldiers in harm's way if they don't know how they will react. The incident with this commander was a good lesson for me. We need to know how we will react during intensive spiritual warfare and even during the collapse of our societal structures and economy. Knowing ourselves is a vital part of preparation in the end times.

Knowing yourself means understanding your strengths, weaknesses, stamina, passions and ambitions. It also involves knowing your mental, spiritual, physical and emotional capabilities.

The best way to look at yourself is through the lens of the Word of God. You can find the help you need there. I have found that reading the book of Proverbs gives me wisdom; the psalms give me hope and courage; the gospels give me strength; and Acts gives me courage and inspiration.

Another good practice is linking up with another spiritual warrior. Proverbs 27:17 says, "As iron sharpens iron, so one person sharpens another."

We need each other in ways we often do not understand. No one in the military goes it alone. It takes a team. So it is in the making of a spiritual warrior. This is one of the reasons being involved in groups of believers (church or small groups) is vitally important for our spiritual growth and health.

But in addition to knowing ourselves, we must know our enemy.

## Who Is the Enemy?

A famous battle and its aftermath highlight why it is important to know your enemy.

At the beginning of American involvement in World War II, U.S. Army General George S. Patton, whose discipline, toughness and self-sacrifice elicited pride among his soldiers, succeeded in battle because he knew the tactics and strategies of his enemy, German Field Marshal Erwin Rommel.

Rommel, "the Desert Fox," had decimated U.S. forces in the Battle of Kasserine Pass. The Allied forces at Kasserine were unprepared, improperly trained and lacking in strong leadership. But Patton had gained a great deal of tactical knowledge while training in the deserts of California before going into combat. His staff had already gathered a great deal of intelligence about Rommel, and he was ready. He knew his enemy. And Patton, known affectionately as "Old Blood and Guts," went on to defeat Rommel in North Africa.

You learn early on in your military career that you cannot defeat an enemy you do not know or understand. Who is the enemy? What are his plans and tactics? How do we defeat him? In order to address these questions, we need a strategy and tactics to implement our plan.

In the Army, the primary officer responsible to the commander at the tactical level (the lowest level for units fighting in the field) for knowing the enemy and his capabilities, tactics, strategies, manpower, equipment, culture and morale is the S2. The S2 in tactical units is usually a captain. In higher operational units (such as a division), the S2 is normally a lieutenant colonel. At the highest levels, intelligence officers go up to lieutenant general (three-star).

Every good commander relies heavily on his or her S2 in order to ensure success on the battlefield. The commander wants to know the enemy's strength and the best strategies to defeat him. Patton did not defeat Rommel by himself. He had an entire staff dedicated to gathering intelligence about his adversary.

In today's military, it is the duty of S2 officers to plan intelligence collection operations. They have several resources for this job. Satellites and unmanned aerial vehicles (UAVs) capture images. Signal Intelligence Collectors gather enemy radio communications. Common Ground Station (CGS) analysts use radar to track enemy vehicles. And Human Intelligence Collectors question enemy combatants and civilians. The S2 determines which tool is best for the job and makes it happen.[1]

"The most important mission of combat battalion S2s is to provide their commanders enough timely information to allow them to make critical decisions on the battlefield," U.S.

Army Captain Norman Fuss writes. "While in the field, this mission far outweighs all others. If the S2 succeeds, the battalion is almost always successful; if the S2 fails, the battalion is almost certainly doomed to defeat and the unnecessary loss of American lives."[2]

The U.S. military has learned the hard way, in the first battles of many wars, the importance of knowing your enemy. The book *America's First Battles* by Charles Heller is required reading at the U.S. Army War College in Carlisle, Pennsylvania. It reveals that in nearly every major war, the U.S. has lost the first battle—mostly due to a lack of preparedness, inexperience, and not knowing the enemy and his tactics or strategies.

Chinese general and military strategist Sun Tzu said, "Strategy without tactics is the slowest route to victory. Tactics without strategy is the noise before defeat."[3]

True. If we do not understand the enemy, how can we have a plan to defeat him? If we have a plan and don't put that plan into action, that is the surest path to defeat.

## Understanding Your Enemy

The powers of darkness at the end will multiply exponentially in strength and numbers. We already see this happening across the globe. We must learn to identify the enemy behind the human powers and initiatives. You may think that most global problems are manmade, but I assure you they are not. We need to learn that our real enemies are not corrupt politicians, terrorists or a host of other human adversaries.

Our friend Dr. Robert Jeffress—senior pastor of the 13,000–member First Baptist Church in Dallas, Texas, adjunct professor at Dallas Theological Seminary, and host of the *Pathway to Victory* television show broadcast globally—has some telling observations about the nature of our enemy. He comments:

> It was C. S. Lewis who described the world as "enemy-occupied territory." And I certainly think there is a sense in which we've always needed to be prepared. We face some formidable opposition—sometimes in the form of other people who oppose our faith, governments that are opposed to our faith, and our adversary the devil who is always against us, plus the remnants of our own fallen nature that remain with us. All these things mean we are engaged in spiritual warfare day in and day out.[4]

Jeffress agrees that, just as demons were active during Christ's first coming, there is scriptural justification for the belief that as the Second Coming of Christ approaches, and Satan realizes his time on earth is limited, an increase in satanic attacks against Christians will occur in the form of persecution and other manifestations.

"So we need to be armed," Jeffress says. "Your book uses military terminology. The apostle Paul uses the armor of a Roman soldier. But whatever the metaphor, the truth is real. We need to be prepared for battle."[5]

The reality is, there are terrifying powers behind the scenes manipulating mankind in order to bring about the final showdown at Armageddon. At the beginning of this chapter, we quoted Ephesians 6:12, indicating that our fight is "against the rulers, against the authorities, against the powers of this dark world and against the spiritual forces of evil in the heavenly realms."

The Greek word for *ruler* is *arche*, meaning something that was in the beginning, a first principle, a substance or primal element. *The New American Standard New Testament*

*Greek Lexicon* defines it as "the first place, principality, rule, magistracy; of angels and demons."[6]

The word Archangel comes from the Greek words "arche" (ruler) and "angelos" (messenger), "signifying archangels' dual duties: ruling over the other angels, while also delivering messages from God to human beings."[7]

In addition, there are dark powers that are rulers over demonic hordes in the invisible realm. Entities on God's side and Satan's side have been involved, since his ejection from heaven, in a titanic struggle, and we are caught in the middle.

The principalities Paul mentions are ruling dark lords or powers that possess executive authority, or governmental rule, in this world. They rule kingdoms on earth that stand in opposition to God.

Satan is the chief ruler of this planet, or, as the Bible describes him, "the god of this age" (2 Corinthians 4:4). Satan is the foremost influence on the world scene. He is behind the social and geopolitical events hurling us toward the final showdown between Christ and the Antichrist at the Battle of Armageddon.

These dark forces are lining up the geopolitical players for the final end-times battle. The focal point where biblical prophecies will unfold: the Middle East—more specifically, Jerusalem. Ezekiel 37 and 38 lay out for us the last battle and the major players involved, including Iran (ancient Persia) and Turkey (ancient Asia Minor). This scenario is now unfolding before our very eyes.

Iran's stated vision is to usher in the end of days and their messiah, the Mahdi or "hidden imam," by destroying Israel and conquering the world for Islam. Iran also believes that the "time before the arrival of the Mahdi will also see a great war in Syria and Iraq that will destroy both countries, accompanied by a great fire and 'redness in the sky.'"[8] Iran has infiltrated most of the Middle East with covert operators and military forces.

At present, Turkey has thousands of troops on the border of Syria and has become a hostile foe to Israel. Turkey has stated so in no uncertain terms: "Whoever is on the side of Israel, let everyone know that we are against them. We do not approve of silence on the state terror that Israel blatantly carries out in Palestine."[9]

Iran and Turkey will be key players in the invasion of the Middle East. Turkey will lead Iran, Sudan, Libya and other nations in an invasion of Israel. Ezekiel 38 and 39 pinpoints these countries.

"The contours of the geopolitical landscape as described by the biblical prophets is coming into profound alignment," says our filmmaker friend Joel Richardson. He goes on to say:

One of the profound signs I see is the rise of an Islamicist, nationalistic, antagonistic, aggressive and imperialistic Turkey. I would argue, based on Ezekiel 38–39, Daniel 8, Zechariah 9 and a handful of other passages, that we'd expect to see Turkey arise in the last days as a significant player and leader of the Middle East—and it could actually be the head of the coming coalition or empire of the Antichrist.

Daniel makes it very clear, if the entirety of his prophecy has end-times fulfillment, that we'd also expect to see a regional Iranian invasion essentially of Iraq, Syria and eventually Israel and the whole of the Middle East. In a lot of ways, that's in the process of being fulfilled the past few years. We now have over 40,000 Iranian troops in Syria. They've also essentially taken over a large part of Lebanon through Hezbollah. As the United States continues to tighten the screws, the potential is for them to lash out in desperate measures like a wounded animal.[10]

Given what we will face in the end times, it is vitally important that we understand our real enemies and learn how to engage them in battle.

Retired U.S. Army Major General Robert F. Dees connects military intelligence with spiritual discernment:

> At my command in Korea, we said, "Readiness never takes a day off on freedom's frontier." The point is, readiness never takes a day off for the warrior because we are always at war and we are always the subject of fighting in this eternal struggle. That suggests that it makes sense to be constantly getting ready, being ready and accessing our readiness.
>
> Another important thing is IPB—that's military lingo for Intelligence Preparation of the Battlefield. IPB is a discipline on the intelligence side, so you do everything possible to learn about the enemy. Where is he? How strong is he? How well equipped? What's his mental state? What's his intent and capability? What does the terrain look like? What does the space you're operating in look like, and how will that limit or advantage you?
>
> The analogy to spiritual warfare is using some of these military principles to understand your spiritual adversary, and gaining insight and wisdom about how to deal with that adversary.[11]

## A Closer Look at the Enemy

We have said that we must know and understand the enemy. In fact, we have at least three enemies that must be identified in order to defeat them. Let's take a look at each one.

### Sin

Our first real and lethal enemy is sin. I know it is not fashionable to talk about sin. We talk about "mistakes," misguided judgment, disease (mental and emotional) and imperfections. But not knowing or understanding sin is a mistake and costly blunder for warriors. Sin is what got mankind in trouble in the first place, separating us from God. Remember the Garden of Eden?

> And the LORD God commanded the man, "You are free to eat from any tree in the garden; but you must not eat from the tree of the knowledge of good and evil, for when you eat from it you will certainly die."
>
> Genesis 2:16–17

God told them not to eat of the fruit of the tree of the knowledge of good and evil. What did they do? Eat the fruit. What happened? They died. And so do we. Notice, they did not die physically for another eight hundred years; but the moment they ate the fruit, they died in relationship to God, to each other, and to the world around them.

Sin kills our relationship to God and to each other. Sin is the reason for war, divorce, murder, hatred and all the other toxic ills of mankind. It is the reason there have been only 268 years of peace over the past 3,400 years of history. Sin is insidious.

At first, sin is a blast. Smoking your first joint, taking your first hit of cocaine, engaging for the first time in illicit sex—these and many other firsts can be the thrill of a lifetime. The problem is, over the years what you thought was fantastic now becomes the master. You cannot escape the addiction. It overpowers you and makes you bend the knee and pay homage to it.

> The sinful nature wants to do evil, which is just the opposite of what the Spirit wants. And the Spirit gives us desires that

are the opposite of what the sinful nature desires. These two forces are constantly fighting each other, so you are not free to carry out your good intentions.

Galatians 5:17 NLT

Sin wreaks havoc in this world all the time. We think we need more education, better politics, new governmental systems, better technology, upgraded computers and smartphones, yoga, visions, mysterious revelations, and a host of other nonsense. I know well-educated people who are stone-cold sinners. Sadly, all education does for some people is make them better and smarter at failing God.

Sin, simply stated, is the violation of God's law. Adam and Eve sinned by not obeying His command concerning the tree of the knowledge of good and evil. The truth is, there is only one cure for sin. It is the blood of Jesus.

Jesus died on the cross (another tree) in order to bring us forgiveness of sins and restore our relationship with God. It is not how good a life you have lived, whether you keep the Ten Commandments, or if you gather to yourself all the good deeds in the world. First things first. Without accepting Christ's atonement for your sins, you cannot be a warrior of God. Period.

It is so simple that we want to complicate it. But here it is in plain and simple English in the Bible: "If you declare with your mouth, 'Jesus is Lord,' and believe in your heart that God raised him from the dead, you will be saved" (Romans 10:9).

### The Flesh

The flesh is our second lethal enemy. The flesh, according to the Bible, is not our body, but that part of us that is at war with God. "It is the rebellious, unruly and obstinate part of our inner self that is operative all the time,"[12] writes Monsignor Charles Pope, pastor of Holy Comforter-St. Cyprian in Washington, D.C.

Most believers call this our sin nature. We are born with it. Don't believe me? Go watch a two-year-old throw a temper tantrum because he did not get his way and you will see it firsthand. The Bible clearly defines the flesh in Galatians 5:19–21 (NASB):

> Now the deeds of the flesh are evident, which are: immorality, impurity, sensuality, idolatry, sorcery, enmities, strife, jealousy, outbursts of anger, disputes, dissensions, factions, envying, drunkenness, carousing, and things like these, of which I forewarn you, just as I have forewarned you, that those who practice such things will not inherit the kingdom of God.

How do you defeat this sin nature? You don't. Don't worry—everyone tries and fails all the time. You cannot defeat the flesh with willpower, a plan, a discipleship program, or even self-discipleship. Victory comes only when you turn yourself over to the Holy Spirit every day. "'Not by might nor by power, but by my Spirit,' says the LORD Almighty" (Zechariah 4:6).

There are plenty of self-help books available online or at bookstores. They are able to help make a better you (which, frankly, is not much!), but they never get to the root problem of sin, our sinful nature, or the war within.

Self-help is an "oxymoron" (apparently contradictory terms appearing together) in the sense that you cannot help something that is beyond your ability. The only real and abiding help available to you is through the Holy Spirit. Why did God allow the sin nature to stay with us after salvation? After all, He could have just obliterated it when we made our confession of Christ as Lord. But He chose to leave it within us.

For the past two thousand years, scholars have argued over whether believers retain the sin nature after being saved. We believe the act of becoming holy is both instantaneous in God's eyes, and a lifelong process, so the struggle with sin is real. Why else would Paul write in Galatians 5:16–17:

> So I say, walk by the Spirit, and you will not gratify the desires of the flesh. For the flesh desires what is contrary to the Spirit, and the Spirit what is contrary to the flesh. They are in conflict with each other, so that you are not to do whatever you want.

I think the real reason the sin nature is still in us on this earth is so that we can develop into strong people of God by making daily choices to avoid sin, to refuse to compromise truth, and to follow hard after Christ. Without these daily choices, there is no struggle, no warfare. With them, we face the daily challenge of choosing to please God with our lives.

I have heard many people say they would not have committed the sin Adam and Eve did, but would have chosen instead to eat of the fruit of the tree of life. I believe we have the same choices every day—whether we will follow God or self. We wake up and make choices, good or bad. *What will I do today? Where will I go? How will I behave? Am I okay with going ahead and cutting some corners on my taxes or in that business decision? It will really help me financially.*

Knowing we are at war makes a big difference in how we live. If we believe that life is something to drift through without worrying about how things turn out, then we will live a carefree, me-centered existence. Or if we live by our own wits, we will get through as best we can. Don't be fooled. Most people live as if there are no rules, no consequences, no judgment. After all, if you believe in evolution and all this is accidental, why not live as though there is no tomorrow? That is why the psalmist states, "The fool says in his heart, 'There is no God'" (Psalm 14:1).

### The Devil

Our third real and lethal end-times enemy is the devil.

It is interesting to note that who you think your enemy is may not, in fact, be your real enemy at all. You may think your co-worker, spouse, relative or friend is wrecking your life or causing you misery. But your real enemy is the darkness behind the person, causing him or her to inflict pain in your life.

Some sophisticated people mock Christians who believe in a personal devil. There is darkness and evil in the world, however, in the form of an entity called Satan.

His name was Lucifer, according to the Bible, meaning "light-bearer" or "morning star." The Bible says this about him in Ezekiel 28:12–15:

> "You were the seal of perfection, full of wisdom and perfect in beauty. You were in Eden, the garden of God; every precious stone adorned you: carnelian, chrysolite and emerald, topaz, onyx and jasper, lapis lazuli, turquoise and beryl. Your settings and mountings were made of gold; on the day you were created they were prepared. You were anointed as a guardian cherub, for so I ordained you. You were on the holy mount of God; you walked among the fiery stones. You were blameless in your ways from the day you were created till wickedness was found in you."

God created a perfect, jeweled, beautiful angelic being. We cannot answer why or what caused wickedness to be found in him. We know that he rebelled against God (as we saw in the last chapter) and took one-third of the angels with him in the rebellion (see Revelation 12:4). Talk about *Star Wars!* We know that pride lifted up Lucifer's heart and that he wanted to be higher than God. Look at this description in Isaiah 14:12–15:

> How you have fallen from heaven, morning star, son of the dawn! You have been cast down to the earth, you who once laid low the nations! You said in your heart, "I will ascend to the heavens; I will raise my throne above the stars of God; I will sit enthroned on the mount of assembly, on the utmost heights of Mount Zaphon. I will ascend above the tops of the clouds; I will make myself like the Most High." But you are brought down to the realm of the dead, to the depths of the pit.

After successfully tempting Adam and Eve, God gave Lucifer control of the earth to administer and oversee. This is evident in Scripture with the temptation of Christ in the wilderness:

> Again, the devil took him to a very high mountain and showed him all the kingdoms of the world and their splendor. "All this I will give you," he said, "if you will bow down and worship me." Jesus said to him, "Away from me, Satan! For it is written: 'Worship the Lord your God, and serve him only.'"
>
> Matthew 4:8–10

Jesus rebuked the devil but never disputed his claim of ownership of the earth.

## Defeating the Enemy

Satan is a powerful personal enemy, then, whom we cannot defeat on our own. But Jesus Christ defeated him at the cross and at the resurrection. He told the apostle John, "I am the Living One; I was dead, and now look, I am alive for ever and ever! And I hold the keys of death and Hades" (Revelation 1:18).

For now, however, this planet is still under Satan's full sway. And Revelation 12:11 offers the key to defeating this enemy: "And they overcame him by the blood of the Lamb, and by the word of their testimony; and they loved not their lives unto the death" (KJV).

I know what will *not* defeat Satan: church social programs, special lighting, fog machines, hip music, social media, politics, more education. No, the ultimate weapons God has given us to defeat the enemy are the blood of the Lamb, the word of our own testimony, and a willingness to give up our lives (see Revelation 12:11).

The Word of God used rightly—"correctly [handling] the word of truth," 2 Timothy 2:15—is another powerful weapon in our arsenal. Memorizing and quoting Scripture out loud can have a more devastating effect on our enemy than an M1A2 Abrams battle tank on the battlefield.

Another powerful weapon to use every day is singing songs of faith. Singing praise to God is another form of "the word of our testimony" and one of the most effective ways of ridding your soul of the enemy's oppression and despair.

But even the most lethal equipment does no good unless we train to use it and focus its lethality on our enemies. It does no good to have a rifle or grenade launcher if we do not arm it and fire it at the enemy. So use the truth of the Gospel, the shed blood of Jesus on Calvary, the power of His resurrection, your own testimony of what Christ has done for you, the Word of God, and His praise in your mouth to defeat both internal and external enemies.

The society we live in is not our friend, nor is it a friend of Jesus Christ and His Gospel.

We have more to learn from David about defeating our enemy.

The year: about 1063 BC. The place: the Valley of Elah, fifteen miles southwest of Jerusalem. The armies: Israel under Saul against the Philistines, led by the warrior Goliath, about nine feet tall and wearing about 150 pounds of armor. When the army of Israel was challenged by the giant, no one in the ranks had the courage to face the brash, blasphemous warrior from Gath. Why was it that no one in the vast Israeli army could come up with a solution to defeat this adversary?

In the natural, it was impossible. All those experienced warriors under King Saul took counsel from their fears. After all, who in his right mind would stand up to this monster of a man who was obviously controlled by some fearsome dark forces? No, human knowledge and experience were not going to defeat the giant. David, the young shepherd, had been diligent every day in feeding, caring for and defending his flock against the lion and the bear. But even those were not enough to defeat the forces of darkness.

But David came with something else that nobody had. He had faith in God.

David said to the Philistine, "You come against me with sword and spear and javelin, but I come against you in the name of the Lord Almighty, the God of the armies of Israel, whom you have defied. This day the Lord will deliver you into my hands, and I'll strike you down and cut off your head. This very day I will give the carcasses of the Philistine army to the birds and the wild animals, and the whole world will know that there is a God in Israel. All those gathered here will know that it is not by sword or spear that the LORD saves; for the battle is the LORD's, and he will give all of you into our hands."

1 Samuel 17:45–47

David knew himself and his enemy. He knew that he could not defeat Goliath by himself. God would have to intervene.

Knowing yourself and your enemy is important, but it is also important to know your God. Every time you endeavor to follow hard after God and suit up for battle, there will be obstacles and obstructions—but He will make a way.

In review, let's look at the military and Christian processes of "knowing your enemy" and how you can apply what you have learned in this chapter.

## MILITARY PROCESS OF KNOWING THE ENEMY

* *Requirements.* These are what the commander needs to know in order to defeat the enemy. While the load of information gathered can be overwhelming, the mission is to ensure that the commander gets the right information at the right time and place.
* *Collection.* This is the practical side of gathering intelligence on the enemy. Once requirements and priorities have been established, the intelligence is collected.
* *Processing and exploitation.* Collection produces information that must undergo processing and exploitation before it can be regarded as intelligence and given to analysts. Conversion includes translations, decryption and interpretation.

⋆ *Analysis and production.* Information by itself is not helpful. In this stage, the information collected is analyzed and assessed to see if it is beneficial to present to the commander.

## BELIEVER'S PROCESS OF KNOWING THE ENEMY

⋆ *Requirements.* These are what you need to know in order to defeat the enemy. The load of information can be overwhelming, so be selective in what you read, hear and study. Make the Word of God your primary go-to book to gain insight, clarity and inspiration for your life.

⋆ *Collection.* Once your requirements and priorities have been established, gather great spiritual materials to read, listen to and study. Many good spiritual resources are out there, including the classics. Make study of the end times a priority so you will not be blindsided when end-times events happen. The Bible exhorts you to "correctly [handle] the word of truth" (2 Timothy 2:15). The Bible also says the Bereans "received the message with great eagerness and examined the Scriptures every day to see if what Paul said was true" (Acts 17:11).

⋆ *Processing and exploitation.* A library full of Bibles and great theological and inspirational books does you no good unless you read, study and meditate on its resources. Review your own collection of spiritual resources to ensure that you have at your fingertips the best Bibles, books and study guides. Not every resource is worth keeping. Keep the ones that make the most impact and are worth reading again and again.

⋆ *Analysis and production.* Philippians 4:8–9 tells us that "whatever is true, whatever is noble, whatever is right, whatever is pure, whatever is lovely, whatever is admirable—if anything is excellent or praiseworthy—think about such things." This process must happen if you aspire to warrior status for God.

Acquiring knowledge for its own sake will not benefit you or make you into a warrior. Countless thousands of Bible studies are taking place every day, but how much of that information is applied to change lives? Meditate, analyze, process and then apply these truths to your life—every day.

## STRATEGIC SPIRITUAL EXERCISES

Here are some practical takeaways and exercises to help you defeat your enemies:

1. Review "The Christian Process of Knowing the Enemy" (above) until you are convinced you have it in your soul.
2. Find a quiet place every day to pay attention to God. Remember, we make time for what is truly important to us. David succeeded because he put time into just being with God (see Psalm 63).
3. Study the enemies of your faith intently, as Patton studied Rommel. These enemies may be both internal (fears, addictions, anger, unforgiveness) and external (time, people, stress, money).
4. Find out your priorities in the end times by looking at how you spend your time and money.
5. Determine what obstacles are keeping you from following hard after God.

# 4

# CENTER OF GRAVITY

To achieve victory, we must mass our forces at the hub of all power and movement. The enemy's "center of gravity."

—Carl von Clausewitz, Prussian general

TO BECOME REAL WARRIORS of God in the end times, we must understand our ultimate goals and objectives. Likewise, we must understand the goals and objectives of the enemy.

If we are in this fight to the end, should we not be armed with what aligns with the Word of God? The consequences of not knowing the enemy's objectives will be monumental.

Clausewitz is considered by many in the military as the godfather of modern strategic warfare. His book *Vom Kriege* (*On War*), published in 1832, is a classic in military strategy. It is studied at the prestigious U.S. Army War College in Carlisle, Pennsylvania, which I had the privilege of attending, as well as at many other military colleges around the world. Clausewitz's influence on how we fight today is immeasurable. He will help us understand the strategies of spiritual warfare, so we can leverage his wisdom in the last days.

He created what is known as the center of gravity (COG)—the key element we must understand to win in combat. The COG is the hub of all power and movement on which everything depends. On today's modern battlefield, the COG can be difficult at times to define, but the military must define it in order to achieve victory. Even though the concept is more than two hundred years old, not defining it can lead to ill-fated consequences.[1]

The Army defines a COG as "those characteristics, capabilities, or sources of power from which a military force derives its freedom of action, physical strength, or will to fight."[2] In other words, if you destroy the enemy's COG, you will bring about certain defeat. The COG, to further define it, is that point at which, when you strike it, the enemy collapses in defeat.

While there is one decisive COG that will finally bring an end to the enemy, there can be, at the same time, multiple COGs throughout an enduring war with many fronts. In World War II, for example, the Allies struck the decisive blow to Adolf Hitler in Normandy, France—site of the famous D-Day landing—but there were still other COGs to come in Japan and elsewhere in the Pacific theater.

In setting the conditions for an end-times warrior's victory, we must understand how to focus our spiritual weapons on the enemy's COG.

In the military, the COG can be many things. It can be the enemy's supply lines, his will to fight, even a concept or worldview—whatever the military strikes that, when destroyed, unravels the entire framework.

In World War II, as I said, Hitler's COG was his defensive force in Normandy. Once the Allies gained a foothold on the beaches of Normandy, the whole of Europe opened to them. The reason U.S. Army General Dwight D. Eisenhower put all his available forces on land and sea, all focused on the French beaches, was to deal a death blow to the Third Reich. D-Day paved the way for victory in Europe.

Although it is strictly a military term, the COG has many applications to the corporate world as well as to our personal and spiritual lives.

In the corporate world, a COG could be the bottom line or corporate profits for the year. If the corporate bottom line is not met, a company can experience serious financial difficulties.

In a similar way, one of the COGs in the end times is the rise of the Antichrist. Once the Antichrist rises to power, most of the world will follow him, and he and the false prophet will preside over a world government and global economic and religious systems. When Christ returns, He will defeat the Antichrist, and the false prophet and the world system he ruled over will collapse. Only Jesus Christ can defeat the Antichrist, and when He does, He will have taken out the enemy's COG. When Christ takes out the Antichrist, the war is over.

## A Personal Center of Gravity

I had an experience with a COG-type situation during my military career. I was assigned as the family life chaplain at Fort Campbell in Kentucky, home to the renowned 101st Airborne Division under the leadership of David Petraeus, then a major general. I was responsible for training chaplains in marriage and family counseling, as well as counseling many of the soldiers assigned there.

On my way to Fort Campbell during the summer of 2002, I envisioned overseeing a world-class counseling center worthy of the famed division. Instead, I walked into a run-down World War II–era building, dreary outside and in.

*This has to be the wrong place*, I said to myself. *A dreadful mistake*. But I was wrong. This *was* the building. For it to become a welcoming place for soldiers and their families, we would need a miracle. But how could this happen during a time of tight budgets and higher priorities in the Army? I made it a matter of prayer.

The Lord reminded me that nothing is too hard for Him. After all, wasn't I a warrior for Him? It occurred to me, as I thought and prayed over the next few weeks, that figuring out the COG in this situation was the secret to solving my dilemma. But what *was* the COG in this case?

*God,* I prayed, *what must happen in order for this building to be turned into the kind of place You want it to be?* The Lord seemed to say, as He often does to those who believe, *Get up and move forward and I will break down the barriers that are in the way.*

I sensed that I should visit the Defense Reutilization and Marketing Office (DRMO) where the military keeps its used equipment and furniture. But it was a dead end. All I saw was a bunch of junk as far as the eye could see. As I turned to leave, an older gentleman working there spoke up. He was a tall, heavy-set fellow, slightly bent over, I suppose, from all the years of moving furniture and equipment.

"Chaplain, what are you looking for in here?" he asked.

I told him about my situation and the need for new furniture, rugs, a television and other things to make my building homier. I told him that I planned to repaint and refinish the building's interior so soldiers and their families could have a really nice place for counseling. I think I made him laugh from the way I said it.

I went on to tell him that I had run into major obstacles, and nothing had seemed to work in my battle for victory in this arena. I told him there was nothing at the DRMO I could use. I needed all new stuff. I may even have mentioned trying to find the COG in this fight.

It turned out to be where I was standing! Because suddenly the tide turned.

"Hold on one minute," he said. "Don't be so sure. You've come in here at the right moment because, you see, I'm retiring in thirty days. I'm not supposed to do this, but I'm going to do it anyway."

He told me to follow him. Using the keys in his hand, he opened the gate to heaven—or so it seemed to me.

A few feet from where I had just been standing, with no hope and no chance of accomplishing my mission, I entered a vast warehouse full of new boxed furniture, office equipment and a whole host of other "goodies."

Unbelievably he said, "Now, Chaplain, you walk down these aisles and select anything and everything you want, and I will put it on my delivery truck and deliver it personally to you today."

He got out his clipboard and pencil and followed me down the aisles and marked down everything I wanted. And, true to his word, he delivered it all that day.

As in most military operations, taking the time, thought and strategy to discover the COG is vital and the key to victory. In this case, I had found a furniture warehouse and the man willing to hand over all that new stuff to me. That COG I had been seeking was blown wide open in those few moments, the enemy of hopelessness was defeated, and God shone forth in His glory.

Many times the COG is not clear. It may even be hidden from us until we seek guidance and direction from God. In my case, it was not until I received a prompting to knock on the door of DRMO that I found the COG unknowingly through my obedience to God's direction.

At times, the COG is crystal-clear and we know how to attack and defeat it. At other times the COG is not clear and we need step-by-step guidance from the Lord to achieve victory.

I realize that this story is small potatoes compared to military operations—or what you may be going through right now. But it emphasizes the point that it is important to know and understand what obstacles, barriers, problems and issues need to be defeated in order to achieve victory in your life.

## Center of Gravity in the End Times

The focus of all biblical history, and the focus of the end times, has always been and always will be Jerusalem.

Jerusalem is the COG of end-times biblical prophecy. Why? Jerusalem is one of the most enduring cities in the world. Historians trace its history to about 4000 BC, when the part of Jerusalem called the City of David was inhabited by nomadic shepherds. It became the capital of Israel under King David. It is the capital of Israel today. And is the future capital of the Kingdom of heaven, where the Lord Jesus Christ will rule the universe from His throne.

Satan and his dark lords and authorities know this. That is why Jerusalem has been destroyed at least twice, besieged two dozen times, attacked several dozen times, and captured and recaptured more than forty times.[3]

Revelation 21:1–2 offers a glimpse of the future of Jerusalem:

Then I saw "a new heaven and a new earth," for the first heaven and the first earth had passed away, and there was no longer any sea. I saw the Holy City, the new Jerusalem, coming down out of heaven from God, prepared as a bride beautifully dressed for her husband.

In this Scripture we see the importance of Jerusalem to God. It is His masterpiece—a future reward for believers, a city unmatched in beauty and majesty, the city we will live in with God forever. Hebrews 11:9–10 helps explain the significance of Jerusalem in God's eternal plan:

> By faith [Abraham] made his home in the promised land like a stranger in a foreign country; he lived in tents, as did Isaac and Jacob, who were heirs with him of the same promise. For he was looking forward to the city with foundations, whose architect and builder is God.

Jerusalem is the epicenter of many biblical prophecies about the return of Jesus, the Day of the Lord, and the thousand-year reign of Christ. Not only that, but it is the center of three major world religions: Judaism, Christianity and Islam. Jerusalem is where the final battle will take place (see Zechariah 14:1–3); where Jesus will first set His foot down, on His return to earth (see Zechariah 14:4); where the restored third Temple will be located; and where the Antichrist, in the third Temple, will declare himself to be God (see 2 Thessalonians 2:3–4).

Nations are willing to fight and die over the ability to control this city. Watch the news about Jerusalem, and you will keep in tune with much of what is happening in the end times.

## Our Enemy's Center of Gravity

Just as we must understand our enemy's COGs, we must also understand that the enemy is focused on our COGs in his fight against God, the Jewish people and Christians. If we do not understand how the enemy views our COGs, we will fail in this conflict. In today's world, there are many COGs. The question is where to focus our prayers in this spiritual battle.

We believe there are three major COGs the enemy is targeting in the spiritual war against God, Christians, Jews, society and culture.

### Religious Culture

The first COG is religious culture. Have you noticed the rising hatred for Christians and the growing persecution taking place across the globe? True faith is one of the three COGs in our enemy's fight against God.

Jesus Himself said to one of His disciples, "And I tell you, you are Peter, and on this rock I will build my church, and the gates of hell shall not prevail against it" (Matthew 16:18 ESV). Satan and the gates of hell are attacking the Church of Jesus Christ in ways unheard of in the modern era.

Many today attending Jesus-honoring, Bible-centered churches do not know Jesus well or what the Bible says or how to pray and engage the enemy. The apostasy taking place in the Church worldwide is frightening. Some of our historic denominations no longer believe in the infallible Word of God. Once-biblical churches and denominations are slipping from Scripture and succumbing to heresy and "doctrines of demons" (1 Timothy 4:1). The significant moral decay we are witnessing is largely the result of the once-mighty Church abandoning the authority of Scripture and bowing the knee to unbiblical theology and even paganism. The situation is far more serious than most people realize.

In addition, our friend retired U.S. Army Major General Robert Dees expresses great concern about the decline of the

Church's influence in each of the seven "mountains of culture" or societal influence—religion, family, education, government, media, arts and entertainment, and business. He says:

> I think secular progressives have planted seeds for the last three or four decades that are now sprouting in great abundance. It's as if they're reaching critical mass in our school systems, culture and media. Really, every one of the seven mountains of culture seems to be aflame with secular progressivism. The concern is that we've reached a tipping point.[4]

In response, there is a growing movement to create small groups or "life groups" within larger congregations. This is an important development for spiritual growth, connectivity and relationship-building. If, in the future, severe persecution breaks out in America, these small groups will become like the house churches during the first century, or in Iran or China today.

What is the solution to the departure from Scripture and deteriorating influence and moral free fall? To bring all this to God in prayer and ask for another great awakening. We are not fatalists. God can still intervene even amid apostasy.

At the same time, we believe that time is short and we must act quickly. When God was about to destroy the children of Israel in His anger, Moses intervened on behalf of the people so God would withhold His judgment and spare them. God relented and, on account of Moses, did not destroy Israel (see Exodus 32:11–14).

### Education

Another COG for our enemy is the educational arena. Satan knows how important learning is for children and young adults. For many years there has been an all-out attack on youth in the educational system. The results are predictable—the upheaval, revolt and decimation of society unfolding today.

When I was in college in the mid-1970s, I took a class on human anthropology. Almost the first words out of the professor's mouth were that Adam and Eve are a myth, that the creation account in Genesis never happened, and that evolution has brought us to where we are today. Such challenges on the college or even high school level throw many young people off course and away from their faith.

Revisionist history is now wildly popular, with historical accounts being reinterpreted to bury spiritual causes and connections. Many educational institutions that started out as Bible colleges and seminaries teach naturalistic philosophy, having moved from creation to evolution, from a Bible-centered to a human-centered worldview.

Nor is the Word of God taught in most public schools, even ones that once required Bible reading and a certain degree of biblical literacy. Society has drifted and lost its moorings. Many people do not know what right looks like anymore, reminding us of Judges 21:25: "Everyone did what was right in his own eyes" (NASB).

As believers, we must focus our energies at home to make sure our children are being educated. We must reintroduce Bible study groups and Bible reading in school at all levels. And we must bring education back into churches with innovative solutions for youth. Sunday school used to be a big deal in churches. It still is in some churches. But it has gone by the wayside at many other houses of worship.

### Government

The third and arguably most important COG for our enemy is government. Anyone who reads or watches the news knows that the foundations of many governments are being shaken. As just one example, the U.S. Congress has bitter rivalries within itself; members of the legislative and executive branches are often at odds; the executive and judicial branches are routinely at loggerheads; and ordinary citizens are disheartened and even cynical about government dysfunction.

Satan is taking many of the governments of the world down the wrong path in a hurry. In fact, it is becoming clear that the forces of darkness want to merge the nations into a one-world government in preparation for the Antichrist's rule.

Yet many people fail to grasp just how dangerous globalism and the undermining of democracy really are. Robert Dees asks:

> How close are we and could this happen? Yes, it definitely could happen. Elections make a difference; leaders make a difference. So to say whether these things are going to happen, we the people have to vote with our feet, have some backbone. You and I have to be messengers—prophets, if you will—to our decadent culture; and prayerfully people will awaken in order to get themselves ready.[5]

## The Believer's Center of Gravity

Believers have COGs, not only in our spiritual lives but also in our personal lives.

The COG for the believer's spiritual life is not the four walls of the building where we worship on Saturdays and Sundays; it is Jesus Christ. While people and things will fail us, Christ will never fail us. As my good friend retired U.S. Army Chaplain Rod Mills says, "Christ is not our priority;

He is our everything, the center of all our being." The Bible declares that He is the very center of the universe:

> The Son is the image of the invisible God, the firstborn over all creation. For in him all things were created: things in heaven and on earth, visible and invisible, whether thrones or powers or rulers or authorities; all things have been created through him and for him. He is before all things, and in him all things hold together.
>
> Colossians 1:15–17

Now let's look at our personal COG. The center of gravity in our personal lives is, frankly, our relationships. These relationships include our relationship to God, our family and our friends.

The enemy has waged a fierce campaign against marriage and family inside and outside the Church, including pastors and their families. Countless lives have been disrupted and damaged by the one whom Jesus said came here to "steal and kill and destroy" (John 10:10). The cost, in terms of brokenness, health, depression and finances, is immeasurable.

So what do we do with our understanding of our center of gravity, and how do we apply it to our lives in these last days? First, after recognizing what the COG is and where it needs to be applied, we must focus the weapons of our warfare with laser-like precision.

Again, our primary COG is Jesus. We get distracted by many other "important" things in life, but the Person and work of Christ must be the very center of our attention. No other priority is higher. This means that, throughout the day, we are in constant communion with Him. He is the first Person we ask questions of and receive answers from. We praise Him throughout the day and consult Him in the night.

The distractions are from our enemy. Against them we use the weapons of our warfare that God has given us. Among many, our primary weapon, like the infantry's rifle, is prayer. Other weapons of our warfare include praise, the study and use of the Word of God, fasting, solitude and fellowship with other believers.

Our collective and individual prayers need to bombard heaven continually on behalf of nations, cities, towns, churches and individuals. We need to target those around us who need deliverance and freedom from bondage. We must ask God to open the eyes, ears and minds of those entangled with the corruption of this world system.

A perfect example of this kind of COG warfare is found in Daniel 9. Daniel, a Jewish exile and one of the highest-ranking administrators in Babylon under King Darius, son of Xerxes, "understood from the Scriptures, according to the word of the LORD given to Jeremiah the prophet, that the desolation of Jerusalem would last seventy years" (Daniel 9:2). So, knowing the timing of the Jews' return to Jerusalem from exile, he approached the Lord with fasting and in sackcloth and ashes, praying this powerful, persistent and specific prayer:

> "Lord, the great and awesome God, who keeps his covenant of love with those who love him and keep his commandments, we have sinned and done wrong. We have been wicked and have rebelled; we have turned away from your commands and laws. We have not listened to your servants the prophets, who spoke in your name to our kings, our princes and our ancestors, and to all the people of the land.
>
> "Lord, you are righteous, but this day we are covered with shame—the people of Judah and the inhabitants of Jerusalem and all Israel, both near and far, in all the countries where you have scattered us because of our unfaithfulness to you. We and our kings, our princes and our ancestors are

covered with shame, LORD, because we have sinned against you. The Lord our God is merciful and forgiving, even though we have rebelled against him; we have not obeyed the LORD our God or kept the laws he gave us through his servants the prophets. All Israel has transgressed your law and turned away, refusing to obey you.

"Therefore the curses and sworn judgments written in the Law of Moses, the servant of God, have been poured out on us, because we have sinned against you. You have fulfilled the words spoken against us and against our rulers by bringing on us great disaster. Under the whole heaven nothing has ever been done like what has been done to Jerusalem. Just as it is written in the Law of Moses, all this disaster has come on us, yet we have not sought the favor of the LORD our God by turning from our sins and giving attention to your truth. The LORD did not hesitate to bring the disaster on us, for the LORD our God is righteous in everything he does; yet we have not obeyed him.

"Now, Lord our God, who brought your people out of Egypt with a mighty hand and who made for yourself a name that endures to this day, we have sinned, we have done wrong. Lord, in keeping with all your righteous acts, turn away your anger and your wrath from Jerusalem, your city, your holy hill. Our sins and the iniquities of our ancestors have made Jerusalem and your people an object of scorn to all those around us.

"Now, our God, hear the prayers and petitions of your servant. For your sake, Lord, look with favor on your desolate sanctuary. Give ear, our God, and hear; open your eyes and see the desolation of the city that bears your Name. We do not make requests of you because we are righteous, but because of your great mercy. Lord, listen! Lord, forgive! Lord, hear and act! For your sake, my God, do not delay, because your city and your people bear your Name."

verses 4–19

Daniel's people were in captivity for their past sins and rebellion against God. Daniel knew Jeremiah's prophecy—that seventy years had passed and that they were to return to their homeland. But their return was not automatic. So God moved Daniel to get down to the nitty-gritty of prayer and repentance on behalf of the people for their release from captivity.

Now it is our turn. Where Daniel was is where we need to be today. This book is a call for believers worldwide to unite to ask God for a mighty outpouring of His Spirit to prepare us for the chaos and delusion that lie ahead, and for the rise of the Antichrist. We need, most of all, to pray and prepare to be warriors of God in the end times. Many, like Daniel, recognize the "times and the seasons" (1 Thessalonians 5:1 kjv) we are in. There is no doubt we are in the last days.

A recent LifeWay Research poll found that nearly nine in ten pastors see at least some current events matching the events Jesus said would occur shortly before He returns to earth. There was a near-consensus that the end times have finally arrived. The poll found that more than half (56 percent) of pastors expect Jesus to return in their lifetimes.[6]

"For too long many pastors shied away from teaching on birth pains and events leading up to the second coming," said bestselling author Joel Rosenberg during the coronavirus pandemic in 2020. "But the current [situation] demonstrates the need for solid, non-sensational preaching done in a biblical manner."[7]

We are watching the prophetic clock tick down. Israel became a nation in a single day in 1948. Jerusalem is the capital of Israel. Islam is probably the fastest-growing religion in the world. There is a growing possibility of war in the Middle East, even World War III. And the fragile global economy, the rise of globalism, the loss of civil liberties, and a host of other events are setting the stage for the coming of the Antichrist and false prophet.

We should be praying like Daniel: "Lord, forgive our sins, restore our people, reinstate Your glory, lead us to righteousness, rebuild the crumbling Church, and let us once again be a light to this world."

## Understanding the Center of Gravity

The plan below outlines how you can determine your COGs. This process will help you prioritize the most important things in your life. We will show you how the military does it, and then we will show you how believers can do it.

In military lingo: *Ends* are the objectives (your end results). *Ways* are actions to achieve those results. And *means* are the resources required to achieve those results. In the World War II scenario described earlier about the invasion of Normandy, it would go as follows. Ends: Defeat Hitler and his military in Europe. Ways: Invade Normandy and push through to Berlin. Means: All the Allied forces and their logistical support.

Below is the military process of determining the COG for any operation of war. As with all things military, it is a step-by-step process. You can use the same process.

## MILITARY PROCESS TO DETERMINE THE COG[8]

* Identify the desired ends or objectives.
* Identify ways to achieve these ends and select the one that evidence suggests is most likely to work. Then select the most elemental or essential action. That

selection is critical. The ways are critical actions that will achieve the desired ends.

* List the means (critical requirements) needed to enable and execute the ways (critical capabilities).
* Select from the list of means the object that possesses the ways to achieve the end. This selection is the center of gravity.

## BELIEVER'S PROCESS TO DETERMINE THE COG

* Create a list and select those things that are the difference-makers in your life and prioritize them in order of importance. On top of that list should be entering into a more intimate relationship with Jesus. This selection is your center of gravity.
* Identify those things in your life that will be difference-makers or difference-breakers. These are the things that will make you into a warrior for the Kingdom or the things that will prevent you from being that warrior.
* Identify the critical actions that must take place for you to achieve the things you have identified. What must you do differently that you have not done before?
* List the resources (time, money, studies, gatherings with other believers, etc.) that you will need in order to accomplish all that you have identified. Include what is necessary to enable you to perform the ways you have identified.

## STRATEGIC SPIRITUAL EXERCISES

Here are some practical takeaways on employing the center of gravity:

1. Take time to reflect on where you are today and what is most important to you. We always make time for what we think is important.
2. Read and reread the prayer in Daniel 9, praying it to the Lord.
3. Find those things in your life that are keeping you from going to the next level with God, and fix them.
4. What areas in your life has the enemy targeted that are keeping you from growing in faith, love and truth? The Holy Spirit will help you overcome those things.

# 5

# FOG OF WAR

War is the realm of uncertainty; three quarters of the factors on which action in war is based are wrapped in a fog of greater or lesser uncertainty. A sensitive and discriminating judgment is called for; a skilled intelligence to scent out the truth.

—Carl von Clausewitz, Prussian general

For now we see through a glass, darkly.

—1 Corinthians 13:12 KJV

*TWILIGHT, EARLY 1990S, Hohenfels, Germany.* A long, grueling day of training today. Armor battling armor throughout the day since early morning. I direct my assistant to drive us in our Humvee ("high mobility multipurpose wheeled vehicles," a sophisticated upgrade to the old Army Jeep) back to our Tactical Operations Center (TOC), where we will spend the night.

Fog descends, night with it. These are before the days of GPS or other forms of digital communications and mapping.

The fog gets so thick I direct my assistant to stop driving. We will rest in place until morning.

*Knock, knock, knock.* It is early morning, the fog is gone, and light is just coming over the peaks. I barely hear the tapping on the side of my Humvee. It is an "observer controller"—the referee of the training.

"Sir, if I were you, I would get out of here in a hurry," he says.

"What's up?"

"Look in back of you."

I look back with a start. "Holy moly." There, about one hundred fifty yards behind us, is a whole row of tanks getting ready to head our way in a hurry.

"Yeah," he says, "and they're about to leave the LD [Line of Departure] in about twenty minutes. If you're still here, you'll be flattened like a pancake."

"No need to tell me twice, OC. We're gone."

Interesting that when my assistant and I were in the fog, nothing was clear, so I decided to stay put until further light. When the fog lifted, everything became clear. I learned where we were and what was about to happen.

Sometimes the best thing to do is wait until things start to clear up.

## End-Times Fog of War

Make no mistake about it. We are at war and at times it can be unclear and confusing. You have heard of many prophets and prognosticators talking about how they have all the answers. They don't. Nobody does.

Jesus predicted the following about the end times:

> "At that time if anyone says to you, 'Look, here is the Messiah!' or, 'There he is!' do not believe it. For false messiahs

and false prophets will appear and perform great signs and wonders to deceive, if possible, even the elect. See, I have told you ahead of time."

Matthew 24:23–25

We interpret this passage to mean that chaos and confusion will abound in the end times, that there will be a spirit of delusion on this planet unlike anything before—and in many ways it is already here.

The fog of war is defined as the chaos often found on the battlefield. The U.S. Army uses the acronym VUCA, which stands for "volatility, uncertainty, complexity and ambiguity." The U.S. Army War College introduced the concept of VUCA, according to General Maxwell P. Thurman, to describe the volatile, uncertain, complex and multilateral world that emerged out of the Cold War.[1]

War is a complex equation. Life-and-death decisions are made in moments. The world has teetered on the brink of nuclear disaster on many occasions because of the fog of war—for example, in the uncertainty and confusion surrounding the Cuban Missile Crisis in October 1962, when the U.S. and the Soviet Union came to the brink of nuclear war.

In the decades since the development of atomic weapons, the world has come close to world war and nuclear Armageddon on many occasions. Currently the greatest threats to world stability are Iran and North Korea, along with the dominance of Russia and China. The world at any given time can be a moment away from nuclear holocaust, especially amid the fog of fear and uncertainty. It is only the Lord who prevents it from happening until the appointed time(s).

New technologies are coming of age in the end times that add a layer of seriousness in military and civilian affairs that, up until now, has been unknown. One of the military's recent "secret weapons" is the LRAD sound cannon, which was used for crowd control during the Ferguson, Missouri, protests in 2014:

> Capable of projecting voice commands over a distance of 9 kilometers (5.5 mi), a Long-Range Acoustic Device (LRAD) inflicts grievous bodily pain upon anyone within 100 meters (330 ft) of its sound path.[2]

The same technology was presumed to be used in an incident at the U.S. embassy in Cuba in 2015:

> Diplomats deployed to the newly reopened US embassy on this Caribbean island nation started reporting a sudden and permanent loss of hearing. US investigators concluded that the diplomats had been hit with an advanced and unnamed acoustic device that doesn't make any audible sound but causes irreparable damage to the ears and brain of anyone in its path.[3]

Life can be very much like a battlefield when you find yourself in the fog and do not understand what to do next. We firmly believe that in the end times, the fog of war will increase, life will become increasingly difficult, and decisions will be hard to make without the guidance of the Holy Spirit.

## Scripture and Fog of War

Even though about a third of the Bible is prophetic, the Scriptures are not explicit as far as dates and times. In fact, the Lord Himself told us while on earth that even He did not know the day or time of His return: "Of that day and hour no one knows, not even the angels of heaven, but My

Father only" (Matthew 24:36 NKJV). And Paul wrote, "Now we see in a mirror, dimly, but then face to face. Now I know in part, but then I shall know just as I also am known" (1 Corinthians 13:12 NKJV).

The lack of a definitive timetable is part of the fog of war. It is advisable, then, that we not state conjecture dogmatically, throwing out times, dates and theories as if they were fact.

A great biblical story on the fog of war is found in the life of Moses as he was leading Israel out of Egypt after they had been captives in the land for more than four hundred years. Pharaoh and all of Egypt finally wanted the Hebrews to leave their land after ten devastating plagues sent by the Lord through Moses. But the Lord led them into a dead-end—or so they thought. Exodus 14 tells the story:

> Then the LORD said to Moses, "Tell the Israelites to turn back and encamp near Pi Hahiroth, between Migdol and the sea. . . . Pharaoh will think, 'The Israelites are wandering around the land in confusion, hemmed in by the desert.' And I will harden Pharaoh's heart, and he will pursue them. But I will gain glory for myself through Pharaoh and all his army, and the Egyptians will know that I am the LORD." So the Israelites did this.
>
> verses 1–4

Here we see a perfect biblical example of the fog of war well over three thousand years ago. The Hebrews following Moses were understandably upset that he had led them into a trap with nowhere to go—the Red Sea in front of them, the entire Egyptian army behind them and closing in fast.

They were terrified and cried out to the LORD. They said to Moses, "Was it because there were no graves in Egypt that you brought us to the desert to die? What have you done to us by bringing us out of Egypt? Didn't we say to you in Egypt, 'Leave us alone; let us serve the Egyptians'? It would have been better for us to serve the Egyptians than to die in the desert!"

verses 10–12

Put yourself in the Hebrews' place. You are now camped by the Red Sea with the strongest army on earth marching angrily toward you. Might you have fear, confusion and anger toward the leadership? You are now in the fog of war. What do you do? Your only hope is complete dependence on the Lord, so you wait for His direction through Moses.

Moses answered the people, "Do not be afraid. Stand firm and you will see the deliverance the Lord will bring you today. The Egyptians you see today you will never see again. The Lord will fight for you; you need only to be still."

verses 13–14

Now the tables turned. Moses stretched out his hand over the sea, the waters divided, and the people walked through on dry ground. God was fighting for His people, and He threw the Egyptians, literally and figuratively, into the fog of war:

The Egyptians pursued them, and all Pharaoh's horses and chariots and horsemen followed them into the sea. During the last watch of the night the Lord looked down from the pillar of fire and cloud at the Egyptian army and threw it into confusion. He jammed the wheels of their chariots so that they had difficulty driving. And the Egyptians said, "Let's get away from the Israelites! The Lord is fighting for them against Egypt."

verses 23–25

Not one Egyptian survived.

In the end of days there will be times when confusion reigns and we do not have answers. Our dependence must always be on God through the power of the Holy Spirit. He will see us through.

## Micah and the Fog of War

My son, David Micah Giammona, can testify to the fog of war. During the spring of 2003, when he was a private first class (assigned to Company H, 121st Infantry Regiment, Long-Range Surveillance Detachment out of the Georgia Army National Guard), he was on a force protection mission just north of Baghdad, Iraq, for a military intelligence battalion. Their mission was to search for weapons of mass destruction.

My son was manning the M60 machine gun (nicknamed the "pig") atop their Humvee, with five other soldiers inside. As they barreled down the road at 55 or 60 miles per hour and came to an overpass, an explosion from an IED (improvised explosive device) rocked their world. The Humvee lurched to the left up on two wheels, and things for Micah went into slow motion. Shrapnel flew into the front of the vehicle, NCOs (non-commissioned officers) shouted commands, and the rear gunner opened up on the enemy combatants, as they took fire from them as well. The noise was deafening.

Fortunately and miraculously, the Humvee did not roll over, and the driver was able to ram through the ambush and keep going. My son received facial burns and others got hit with shrapnel, but there were no fatalities. Later Micah and other soldiers and NCOs in the vehicle at the time of the attack received the Purple Heart for wounds sustained in combat.

In a subsequent conversation, Micah told me that he understood the fog of war as "confusion, smoke and noise" for those few brief moments that plunged them into chaos. He said all their training kicked in, so that everything he did during and after the ambush was the result of the time spent in preparation for combat. "It was all muscle memory," he said, "since there was no time to think."

May we, too, have such "muscle memory" in days to come.

## MILITARY PRINCIPLES FOR THE FOG OF WAR

The U.S. military uses four fundamental principles to guarantee effective operations in the middle of uncertainty:[4]

* *Training.* The Army has a well-known maxim: "Train as you fight." All military branches place their troops in difficult training cycles and scenarios in order to produce the kind of soldier who will perform well in warfare.

* *Intelligence.* The daily intelligence report to the commander includes the current and near future information on METT-T (Mission, Enemy, Troops available, Terrain and Time)—what we believe the enemy is doing in the near term.

* *Planning.* In the fog of war and times of uncertainty, a well-crafted strategic plan is essential for success. It must incorporate suitable data and facts for a positive outcome.

* *Standardized practices.* Pre-mission inspection checks and rehearsals serve as the foundation in preparing for any mission. Adhering to military procedures is vital because these standards ensure smooth, rapid and

effective execution, even when the plan or conditions change.

## BELIEVER'S PRINCIPLES FOR THE FOG OF WAR

God has given us the requisite power and authority to operate in uncertainty. Following the biblical principles will help you not only to overcome the fog of war in the end times but to walk in the supernatural blessings that God promises us:

* *Training.* In the Kingdom of God we also "train as we fight." Do not waste a single day by not putting into use all the training you have received up to this point. Put on the full armor of God as described in Ephesians 6. Train in godly practices every day as if your life depends on it.

* *Intelligence.* Daily reading and listening to the Word of God, as well as listening to and watching sermons by godly pastors, is the best way of gathering the intelligence you need for the day. Throughout the day listen to and obey the promptings of the Holy Spirit.

* *Planning.* Plan for victory by making godly decisions, being led by and listening to the Holy Spirit, spending time alone with God, and intensely seeking godly counsel.

* *Standardized practices.* Preparation for any mission starts with ensuring that your routine includes the above items on a regular schedule. Following these practices will help ensure smooth, rapid and effective execution of God's plan for your life—even when conditions change.

## STRATEGIC SPIRITUAL EXERCISES

Here are some practical takeaways for living in times of uncertainty:

1. Have an honest talk with God about how you don't know the way ahead but would like to hear from Him about the uncertainty in your life.
2. Don't panic! Read Matthew 8:23–27. Rest assured that Jesus is in the boat of life with you.
3. Give time for your training to take effect. It does not happen overnight, but it will happen.
4. Don't yield to the temptation to make a rushed decision amid the fog. The Bible declares: "Stand still, and see the salvation of the LORD" (Exodus 14:13 KJV).
5. Read Exodus 14 over and over!

# 6

# VISION

Where there is no vision, the people perish.

—Proverbs 29:18 KJV

SO YOU WANT to be a great champion for God? A warrior? Sun Tzu, one of the greatest military strategists in history, believed that "victorious warriors win first and then go to war, while defeated warriors go to war first and then seek to win."[1] He meant that real warriors envision victory before going into battle. They plan to win. They train to win. They win!

We are not talking about the current trends in self-help or positive confession, but what we must do in these last days to envision and become the kinds of warriors God intends us to be. We need this mentality: "If God is for us, who can be against us?" (Romans 8:31). But if we continue to live as if nothing is going to change and nothing is going to happen, then we will reap what we have sown. No, we must live life on the cutting edge, preparing for the last days before the coming of the Lord.

Most people will balk at this, but the truth is, things are changing and will change dramatically over the next few years. We must have vision and understand the multi-domain battle space around us.

## Multi-Domain Battle Space

The U.S. Army calls itself the "most lethal and capable ground combat force in history" and has a vision for the future:

> The Army of 2028 will be ready to deploy, fight, and win decisively against any adversary, anytime and anywhere, in a joint, multi-domain, high-intensity conflict, while simultaneously deterring others and maintaining its ability to conduct irregular warfare. The Army will do this through the deployment of modern manned and unmanned ground combat vehicles, aircraft, sustainment systems, and weapons, coupled with robust combined arms formations and tactics based on a modern warfighting doctrine and centered on exceptional Leaders and Soldiers of unmatched lethality.[2]

The "multi-domain" battle space mentioned above refers to the many environments, or spheres (air, sea, land, space and cyberspace), in which the military must be able to fight. The Army's vision accounts for the developing technologies, strategies and tactics of its adversaries, including near-peer competitors like China and Russia. It can no longer count on advanced technologies such as cruise missiles and unmanned drones to dominate its adversaries as in the past. The Army has discovered that if you are satisfied with the status quo, you will soon fall behind and be at the losing end of warfare.

Likewise, we as believers must be able to fight in multiple dimensions as well: physical, spiritual, financial and emotional. Note well the following message from David G. Perkins, a four-star general and retired commander of the U.S. Army Training and Doctrine Command:

> The world is changing rapidly, and the operating environment is becoming more contested, more lethal, and more complex. Additionally, our peer adversaries are challenging the ability of the U.S. and our allies to deter aggressive actions. These changes are not new endeavors, but how we wage war, the speed and violence of armed conflict, and its global impacts are beyond anything we have seen in the past.[3]

In World War II, armies fought on the battlefield, so the battle space was generally the ground around them. Sometimes the threat came from the air in the form of Luftwaffe (German air force) bombers and fighters, and at other times by sea during naval battles.

Today the battlefield is multidimensional. Instead of the clear battles lines soldiers fought over in World War II, the enemy is all around, as I experienced in the wars in Iraq and Afghanistan.

When you are at war, you must focus your vision on what the battle space looks like. You will not achieve victory if you do not see the battlefield in all its dimensions. As Sun Tzu taught, victorious warriors see the full battlefield and know what must be done. That is why they are winners—because they know ahead of time what it takes to defeat the enemy.

## Warriors with Vision

Spiritual warfare requires understanding. We do not just wake up, take a shower, put our clothes on, eat breakfast and go blithely about our day without envisioning and understanding the real battle space—the spiritual battle-field roiling all around us. If we do not understand the tactics, techniques and procedures of the enemy, we will stay defeated.

We must also understand the magnitude of the powerful spiritual forces we are up against. If we have a weakness, a besetting sin, an addiction; if we are not reading the Word of God, praying and fasting regularly; if we are not connected to God all day in prayer—we will lose the spiritual battle. That is why we must look to Scripture for examples of warriors with vision to model our spiritual lives after.

### David

David defeated Goliath as a young man, even before he put that stone into his sling and cast it at the giant. He had the battle skills. He had practiced most of his life. He understood the battle space and ran, not walked, to the line of battle. He knew what he was going up against. And he had vision. He knew in his heart he could defeat Goliath. How did he know? Because he had confidence in his God.

"David was a perfect model of a believer," says Dr. Robert Jeffress, senior pastor of First Baptist Church in Dallas.

> He's what I'd call a velvet-covered brick. He had the right combination of toughness and tenderness. David was a musician. But he was tough as nails when it came to doing battle. He had some memorable failures in his life. Yet he prayed to God to wash him and to make him clean again. I think that's probably the most important characteristic of a warrior for Christ—to be forgiven and to want to live a godly life.[4]

## *Paul*

Vision changed everything for a first-century Pharisee named Saul, who was traveling to Damascus to imprison believers in Jesus.

As he neared Damascus on his journey, suddenly a light from heaven flashed around him. He fell to the ground and heard a voice say to him, "Saul, Saul, why do you persecute me?"

"Who are you, Lord?" Saul asked.

"I am Jesus, whom you are persecuting," he replied. "Now get up and go into the city, and you will be told what you must do."

Acts 9:3–6

And Saul, temporarily blinded, went.

How did a persecutor of the Church have an instantaneous and complete turnaround? Because he had encountered Jesus, and that vision changed his life. Saul, who became Paul, went from a hyper-religious murderous zealot to arguably the greatest apostle, who wrote almost half the books in the New Testament.

He had vision. He knew there would be both physical and spiritual battles, battles on land and sea, in the spirit and in the flesh, with other believers, and with those opposed to the Gospel. But he said this just before he left this earth:

I have fought a good fight, I have finished my course, and I have kept the faith. From now on a crown of righteousness is laid up for me, which the Lord, the righteous Judge, will give me on that Day, and not only to me but also to all who have loved His appearing.

2 Timothy 4:7–8 MEV

## *Present Day*

Vision can change your life, but it must come from the Lord. Some say you can become whatever you want to be. Sorry, not true, especially for the believer warrior. The apostle James offers believers this admonition:

> You do not even know what will happen tomorrow. What is your life? You are a mist that appears for a little while and then vanishes. Instead, you ought to say, "If it is the Lord's will, we will live and do this or that."
>
> James 4:14–15

The Lord promises to guide you if you trust fully in Him. He instills vision over the course of time. It will not always happen in the same way, but God is faithful and will lead you in the way you should go. He promises, "Call to me and I will answer you, and will tell you great and hidden things that you have not known" (Jeremiah 33:3 ESV).

## My Call

In August 1985 I was in line to register for my first semester's tuition at Golden Gate Baptist Theological Seminary in the Bay Area—although I did not have a dime to my name.

A few months prior I had been sitting at a U.S. Marine Corps boot camp graduation at Camp Pendleton in Southern California to watch my brother-in-law graduate with honors. As I watched with intensity the rigor, discipline, precision and esprit de corps of these Marines, I was in awe. It dawned on me that they had mastered the fundamentals of their discipline. I was hooked.

## A Voice

As I watched, a voice out of the blue told me that I was to join the military. I looked around, right in the graduation, to see who was talking to me, but no one was there. I knew this voice, the still, small voice that many times we miss because we are too busy with all the noise in our lives. It was a turning point in my life. A new vision was coming. (I am not given to hearing voices, so don't draw any conclusions just yet! You can do that later.)

What was I to do with this new information? Tell my wife, Esther, sitting next to me, or keep it to myself? I decided the latter was the better part of valor.

The next week I went to the Army recruiter's station near our apartment in Sacramento, California, and asked some basic questions. The recruiter asked me some basic questions as well: What are your interests, education, etc.? I told him I was a college graduate with a degree in music. There are musicians in the Army, he told me, but mostly enlisted soldiers, not officers. I also told him I was a licensed minister. Then he said, "Sir, that's a no-brainer. Why don't you become a chaplain?"

"What's a chaplain?"

"They minister to our military. Here's the phone number to our regional chaplain recruiter in San Francisco."

The rest is history.

Well, at least it is *my* history, but getting from here to there was a long process in fulfilling the vision of becoming a chaplain in the U.S. Army: four years in college, three years in seminary, several years in preparation to be ordained as a minister, and then the basic chaplain course. Thirty-two years later, I am a full colonel senior chaplain. But this was not the end, only the beginning.

### A Vision

Shortly before my retirement in June 2018, Esther and I drove to one of our favorite spots to pray—The Coming King Sculpture Prayer Garden in Kerrville, Texas—where I had an experience unlike any I have had in my life.

Up in the air, several thousand feet above me in a clear, blue Texas sky, I saw a cloud, and it was the Lion of the tribe of Judah. I mean, the mane, the hair, the eyes, the nose, everything, looking straight at me. The Lord spoke through the cloud and said to me, "I am the Lion from the tribe of Judah. I'm about to return. Prepare the Church and warn the world this is going to happen."

I returned to the car where I had left Esther praying and waiting for me. I was visibly shaken and related to her what happened. We rejoiced in the fact that the Lord would show us what He wanted us to do.

This awe-inspiring, life-changing spiritual encounter occurred exactly when it needed to happen, shortly before my retirement from the Army, to launch me into the next phase of my life. I responded to Jesus' call to go out and wake up the Church and the world to what is about to happen on this planet.

## End-Times Vision

During the years of my service as a chaplain, God was preparing me to be a literal warrior in the Army for the Kingdom of God. It was there that I learned and lived the principles I am now sharing with you. And the vision in Kerrville, Texas, persuaded me that things on this planet are about to change drastically, and that we need to prepare for coming earth-shattering events. This book you are reading is one of the results.

Satan and his dark lords and authorities (see Ephesians 6:12), along with those who have rejected Christ as Savior, also have a vision for this world in these last days. The vision of the evil one is spelled out in Revelation 13:1–4:

> The dragon stood on the shore of the sea. And I saw a beast coming out of the sea. It had ten horns and seven heads, with ten crowns on its horns, and on each head a blasphemous name. The beast I saw resembled a leopard, but had feet like those of a bear and a mouth like that of a lion. The dragon gave the beast his power and his throne and great authority. One of the heads of the beast seemed to have had a fatal wound, but the fatal wound had been healed. The whole world was filled with wonder and followed the beast. People worshiped the dragon because he had given authority to the beast, and they also worshiped the beast and asked, "Who is like the beast? Who can wage war against it?"

The end-times vision of Satan, who tries to mimic everything Christ has done for mankind, is to indwell a human being and rule the earth through this person, aptly named the Antichrist. This parallels God sending Jesus as the Messiah who, in the fullness of time, will rule the world from Jerusalem.

The Bible is filled with prophecy about the Antichrist, and for good reason: He will dominate the world. People will be so enthralled with this person that they will worship him and brag about his powers and authority.

Much as Hitler rose out of the chaos of economic hyperinflation in Germany during the Great Depression, when people were literally carting around wheelbarrows full of German marks to buy groceries,[5] the Antichrist will rise up out of economic, religious, social and governmental upheaval—"out of the sea" (Revelation 13:1)—to provide answers to unsolvable problems.

## A Modern-Day Superhero?

Our world is being prepared in many ways for the coming of this man. Notice the proliferation of vastly popular films about superheroes, including movies like *The Avengers* and many others based on characters from Marvel Comics, as well as films about alien invasions, end-of-the-world scenarios and zombies. Why? We are being conditioned and led down a path for the revelation of the man with superpowers—the Antichrist.

Our filmmaker friend Joel Richardson believes that, although we are closer to the emergence of the Antichrist than at any time before, "there are still a few things that need to unfold first before he emerges." He continues:

> I think there will be some significant, regional Middle Eastern wars that will take place that will put Israel and many of the Middle Eastern nations in a peculiar and difficult position, in which they will be willing to engage in some type of regional security alliance—the "covenant with death" described in Isaiah 28:15, and also in Daniel 9, which talks about the "prince who is to come" entering into a covenant with "many." I believe the Antichrist will enter into some sort of security alliance with Israel, which again is alluded to through some prophecies in Isaiah where Judah is warned not to enter into a security alliance with Egypt to protect themselves from the invasion of Nebuchadnezzar. That becomes the sort of historical shadow, or type or pattern, of what Israel will do in the last days with the Antichrist.[6]

Many people wonder if the Antichrist will control the whole world or just the region where he is located. We have studied and explored this question intently. One thing is for certain: The Antichrist will have a severe impact over the entire world.

Because of the signs [the second beast] was given power to perform on behalf of the first beast, it deceived the inhabitants of the earth. It ordered them to set up an image in honor of the beast who was wounded by the sword and yet lived. The second beast was given power to give breath to the image of the first beast, so that the image could speak and cause all who refused to worship the image to be killed. It also forced all people, great and small, rich and poor, free and slave, to receive a mark on their right hands or on their foreheads, so that they could not buy or sell unless they had the mark, which is the name of the beast or the number of its name.

Revelation 13:14–17

Is John the Revelator telling us that these "inhabitants of the earth" are all people of one region (perhaps the Middle East), or the entire planet? Whether the Antichrist's power is regional or global, he will undoubtedly affect the entire planet. All will experience his effects since it is Satan's plan to rule the world through this human interface.

The mark of the Beast has been written about in many books and articles. For the first time in history, the technologies to create the mark of the Beast are in existence today and will only infiltrate our lives more as time goes on.

Today's smartphones will be considered primitive in the next few years as microtechnology shrinks communication into what will be implanted in us. Tattoos will be melded with these technologies to be even more popular and fashionable. This article from *Allure* magazine suggests what is taking place:

Chris Harrison, a professor of computer science at Carnegie Mellon University's Human-Computer Interaction Institute, has been working on a similar idea since 2009. "People want to do more sophisticated things on mobile phones. And the industrial answer seemed to be: Let's put bigger and bigger screens on them," he says. "That only works up to a point. Why don't we just forget the screen entirely? Why not use the skin? Instead of the three-and-a-half-inch iPhone, why not have the 20-inch arm bone?" So, Harrison created OmniTouch (also in collaboration with Microsoft), a device worn on the shoulder that would project your phone interface onto your palm. A depth-sensitive camera picked up when and where you tapped on your skin, so the projection reacted with it. "The invention of smartphones enabled the creation of all these ideas and apps and services. Imagine what that will be like for the body," Harrison says.[7]

These technologies are following us into the workplace. Consider the implications in your own life as revealed in this *Wall Street Journal* story:

> For many employees, the workday starts by swiping a plastic ID card to enter the office. But employers can't always be sure who's holding the card. That humble ID badge is starting to be replaced by biometric identification systems, microchip implants and tools that monitor workers' gaits or typing habits—technologies that might not only make workplaces more secure and easier to navigate but also generate personalized health and productivity data.[8]

Over the centuries many leaders have been identified as the Antichrist, including the Roman emperor Nero, various popes, Hitler, Italian dictator Benito Mussolini, Soviet Union dictator Joseph Stalin and many others. Some of these figures may have exhibited Antichrist tendencies, but 1 John 2:18 (NKJV) tells us that "many antichrists have come, by which we know that it is the last hour." Remember, too, the Bible is Middle East–centric, so he will most likely be from that part of the world.

The Bible tells us that the Beast, or Antichrist, will have miraculous powers, persuasive powers of speech, shrewdness beyond belief, and extraordinary negotiating skills. Satan will enter the Antichrist and become one with this human; that is the reason for his powers. The purpose behind all this: Satan's rule of the world. Consider the words of theologian Arthur W. Pink:

> "That day shall not come, except there come a falling away [the Apostasy] first, and that Man of Sin be revealed, the *Son of Perdition*" (2 Thessalonians 2:3). Nothing could be plainer than this. Here the Antichrist is expressly declared to be superhuman—"the Son of Perdition." Just as the Christ is the Son of God, so Antichrist will be the son of Satan. Just as in the Christ dwelt all the fullness of the Godhead bodily, and just as Christ could say, "He that hath seen Me, have seen the Father," so the Antichrist will be the full and final embodiment of the Devil. He will not only be the incarnation of the Devil, but the consummation of his wickedness and power.[9]

We will talk more about the Beast, and his mark, in the next chapter.

## A Vision for the End Times

How do you live a normal life given all the disconcerting things taking place in our world today? You must still go to school or work, pay your bills, clean your house, and perform a host of other everyday activities that make up life for the average person. Jesus said it would be so:

"As it was in the days of Noah, so it will be at the coming of the Son of Man. For in the days before the flood, people were eating and drinking, marrying and giving in marriage, up to the day Noah entered the ark; and they knew nothing about what would happen until the flood came and took them all away. That is how it will be at the coming of the Son of Man."

Matthew 24:37–39

Some civilians think that, in the military, there is constant warfare, excitement and an adrenaline rush. But even during combat, nothing could be further from the truth. There are many days of boredom, cleaning weapons, routine maintenance, training, practice and just plain mundane stuff. All that "stuff," however, helps prepare you for the moments when you find yourself in the thick of it. Without preparation and training, there is no victory. Success in the end times is all about preparation, steadfastness and patience.

Here are some insights into the Army vision for 2028 and the believer's vision for the end times.

## MILITARY FUTURE VISION

* *Man.* Add personnel, growing the force to more than 500,000 soldiers.
* *Organize.* Ensure that war-fighting formations have enough infantry, armor, engineers, artillery and air defense assets.
* *Train.* Focus on high-intensity conflict, with an emphasis on operating in dense urban terrain.
* *Equip.* Modernize the force by reforming the current system. Develop autonomous systems, artificial

intelligence and robotics to make soldiers more effective.

* *Lead*. Develop smart, thoughtful, innovative leaders.

## BELIEVER'S END-TIMES VISION

* *Man*. Grow in grace and power in order to meet the enemy head on. Grow the Church numerically with discipled believers. Add to our numbers warriors for God.

* *Organize*. Join a small group focused on training and discipling you as a believer. Ensure that you have organized your life purpose around Jesus Christ.

* *Train*. Focus on learning and memorizing passages of the Word of God that will strengthen you, and add books to your library that will inspire your walk with the Lord and prepare you for the end times.

* *Equip*. Get around believers, Bible studies, colleges and online programs that will equip you as if your life depends on it.

* *Lead*. Become all that God has for you. Discover your gifts by asking thoughtful leaders what they see in you. Ask Jesus for the wisdom to develop your leadership capabilities and capacity.

## STRATEGIC SPIRITUAL EXERCISES

Here are some practical takeaways for creating a vision for the last days:

1. Ask God to give you wisdom that pertains to building vision in your life. Read wisdom Scriptures,

including James 1:5, Proverbs 1:7, Proverbs 2, Psalm 111:10 and Ecclesiastes 7:12.

2. Find a spiritual mentor who will inspire, invigorate and instigate vision in your life.

3. Study the life of the apostle Paul in the book of Acts and in his New Testament letters. How did he maintain his vision amid stress and persecution?

4. Develop a library (digital or paper) of books that speak to you regarding vision and insight. These authors might include C. S. Lewis, Brother Lawrence, J. I. Packer, John Bunyan and many more.

5. Determine what God has for you to accomplish and then set about doing just that.

# 7

# COURAGE

"Have I not commanded you? Be strong and courageous. Do not be afraid; do not be discouraged, for the LORD your God will be with you wherever you go."

—Joshua 1:9

SUMMER 2005, *early morning, Victory Base Complex, Iraq*. The fighting in and around Baghdad is intense. My assistant and I hitch a ride on a Sikorsky UH-60 Black Hawk helicopter. It is my first helicopter ride into a hot combat zone.

We are part of a group of six Black Hawks flying a routine mission from Victory Base to the Green Zone in the heart of Baghdad to check on the morale of our troops scattered around the area. We are flying low and I am looking down over the city, seeing many explosions along the route. (Later I learn that more than six hundred civilian casualties are taking place that morning.)

Then I notice flares shooting out of our Black Hawk and the others. I hear *ting, ting, ting*—what sounds like a small hammer hitting our bird. It is enemy small arms fire from below. Our door gunner opens up with his M60D machine gun, spraying the ground below.

I think, *This looks like something out of a movie.* Then I realize this is no movie. We may not make it back to base camp. Fear and adrenaline pump through me.

But we land on schedule, and I am picked up in an armored Land Cruiser and taken to the Green Zone. Once there we come under mortar attack and seek cover as quickly as possible. We have gone from the frying pan into the fire.

I discover in these moments that courage is not the absence of fear. It is the ability to continue the mission no matter what, because that is what God has called me to do. In these moments, training and instincts take over. I must be prepared for what life throws at me. And the most important thing is reliance on God. Whether I live or die, He will see me through.

## When Fear Meets Courage

Not all days in the military are like this one, but it is good to know that we serve a powerful God who watches over us night and day, no matter what. God will provide the courage we need when we need it, not before or after. The key is to trust Him, not ourselves.

We are all in need of courage because we will face seemingly insurmountable trials in the days ahead. The greater the problem, the more courage we need to face it. With God's grace, we will overcome.

Here is the U.S. Army's definition of personal courage:

> With physical courage, it is a matter of enduring physical duress and at times risking personal safety. Facing moral fear or adversity may be a long, slow process of continuing

forward on the right path, especially if taking those actions is not popular with others. You can build your personal courage by daily standing up for and acting upon the things that you know are honorable.[1]

In the Army, there is a running joke that goes like this: "A Medal of Honor winner is someone who was in the wrong place at the wrong time." We hold the highest respect for our Medal of Honor winners, no doubt. But the joke reveals the truth that most of us do not want to be in harm's way unless it is necessary and critically vital to our national security.

Courage is mandatory, not optional, for the warrior of God. There is mounting pressure from society to conform to the world's politically correct standards. The current yardstick says that to impose your beliefs on anyone else is arrogance or worse. We need to be strong and of good courage to stand up for our beliefs now, and to face the Antichrist and his hordes in the last days.

Jesus gives the alternatives:

> "To the thirsty I will give water without cost from the spring of the water of life. Those who are victorious will inherit all this, and I will be their God and they will be my children. But the cowardly, the unbelieving, the vile, the murderers, the sexually immoral, those who practice magic arts, the idolaters and all liars—they will be consigned to the fiery lake of burning sulfur. This is the second death."
>
> Revelation 21:6–8

If we decide to receive the mark of the Beast (which we discussed in the last chapter), we will not enter the New Jerusalem or the Kingdom of heaven; our fate will be the lake of fire. But it takes courage even today to stand up to those who are antagonistic to the Gospel of Jesus Christ. Courage is a vital part of who we are in Christ.

Courage is not the absence of fear; it is the ability to keep going in the face of opposition, even though you are afraid. That is why the military trains constantly—so that, as my son Micah experienced in Iraq, your instincts take over when the going gets tough.

## Courage Under Persecution

"We're told in Scripture very clearly that there's a coming conflict," says my friend Colonel Peter Brzezinski, U.S. Army chaplain at Fort Sam Houston in Texas. He continues:

> Depending on your theology, I think we're going through some of those trials now. In fact, today there are more Christians suffering persecution than at any time in history. We're somewhat immune to it in the West, but I think that is changing quickly. And so, as the day draws near for the Lord to return, we need to be prepared and understand what Scripture says about how to best stand firm in these last days and not be swept away by the evil tide. That time is approaching quickly.[2]

More and more believers are being accused of spreading hate. In countries around the world, Christian ministers and groups are routinely arrested on charges of "hate speech" for communicating what the Bible calls sin.[3]

Sometimes we *do* express hate or speak out without love and discretion. But far more often, Christians experience persecution simply for living and expressing their beliefs. In the not-too-distant future, could believers in the West face jail for hate crimes? This is what the early Christians faced in the Roman Empire. Their persecution, which scattered them to other parts of the region, began in Jerusalem with the stoning of Stephen.

He had preached Jesus, confronted apostasy, stood against the moral and religious climate of the day, and stirred up so much animosity in the hearts of religious leaders that he was stoned to death. As he died, "he fell on his knees and cried out, 'Lord, do not hold this sin against them'" (Acts 7:60)—a prime example of courage and love under fire.

Hatred of Christians in Rome continued in the first century under the Roman emperor Nero. The underlying problem was the refusal of Christians to worship pagan gods and the emperor, who was considered a deity. Followers of Jesus claimed to belong to another Kingdom, while Nero saw them as traitors to the Empire. Persecution lasted in Rome until around 313 AD, when Constantine, the first emperor to profess Christianity, approved the Edict of Milan, establishing toleration for Christians in the Roman Empire.[4]

Today, as we have noted, believers in a record number of nations are experiencing persecution, abuse and even genocide at the hands of dictators and authoritarian regimes. Open Doors estimates that one in nine, or 245 million, of the world's 2.5 billion Christians experience high levels of persecution.[5] Astonishingly it is estimated that more Christians have died for their faith over the last century than in all the other centuries of Church history combined.

Frank J. Gaffney, president and chief executive officer of Save the Persecuted Christians, says:

> If you think of the worst atrocities in the history of the world—what Pol Pot did in Cambodia, what Adolf Hitler did in the Third Reich, what Joseph Stalin did in the Soviet Union, what Mao Zedong did in China, and if you put the

numbers of people that they killed together, it would pale by comparison with the number of lives being destroyed—not in every case people being killed, but lives being destroyed—around the world today.[6]

Do not think for one moment that this kind of persecution cannot happen in the West. It has already started. Floodgates of lawlessness, immorality and corruption have been swung wide open. What used to be called immoral, indecent and ungodly has now become the populist movement of our time.

Many in the Bible stood up for righteousness and morality in the face of adversity. Given what's happening today, one in particular stands out.

## Joshua and Courage

Twelve men were sent by Moses to spy out the land of Canaan while the Israelites were in the desert. Was the land good? Was the soil fertile? Were the residents to be overcome powerful? Ten of the spies told Moses—and everyone in Israel's camp—that the land was good, but that there was no way they could defeat the people and giants who lived there.

Joshua and Caleb were the only two spies with a good report. "Do not be afraid of the people of the land," they said, "because we will devour them. Their protection is gone, but the LORD is with us. Do not be afraid of them" (Numbers 14:9).

Tragically, the people believed the ten, not the two; and it would be forty years before the Israelites were allowed to enter the land. What happened to the ten spies? They died in the wilderness along with the rest of the Israelites who refused to believe God's promises. In Numbers 14:30–34 He states:

"Not one of you will enter the land I swore with uplifted hand to make your home, except Caleb son of Jephunneh and Joshua son of Nun. As for your children that you said would be taken as plunder, I will bring them in to enjoy the land you have rejected. But as for you, your bodies will fall in this wilderness. Your children will be shepherds here for forty years, suffering for your unfaithfulness, until the last of your bodies lies in the wilderness. For forty years—one year for each of the forty days you explored the land—you will suffer for your sins and know what it is like to have me against you."

It is safer to follow the Lord than anyone else. Even though the grumblers among the Israelites thought they were playing it safe, they died in the wilderness, while Joshua and Caleb lived on to see the Promised Land.

Where did Joshua find the courage to face the giants who lived there? He was a true warrior whom God had selected to lead the nation of Israel into the land after the death of Moses—and into combat against the fierce people of Canaan. As we noted at the beginning of this chapter, God encouraged Joshua to "be strong and courageous. Do not be afraid; do not be discouraged, for the Lord your God will be with you wherever you go" (Joshua 1:9).

Joshua learned courage from his mentor Moses, who helped him embark on his journey. Joshua had seen what Moses went through for more than forty years in the desert after liberating his people from slavery in Egypt.

In truth, there was no need for God to tell him not to fear if Joshua was not afraid. But even though he was afraid, he chose not to take counsel of his fears. Instead he chose to depend upon God, who could (and did!) perform miracles on his behalf. Likewise we can learn to be brave as we watch others who exhibit godly courage.

## Training for Courage

In this end-times age, fear is prevalent throughout the world and will only intensify in the years ahead. So, determine ahead of time to be trained and ready with the full armor of God as your defense. We will look at the pieces of armor listed in Ephesians 6 in the next section of this chapter.

What kinds of courage are needed?

### Courage to Endure

If you think it will be safer to follow the Antichrist during the Tribulation than to take a stand with the Lord Jesus Christ, think again. Revelation 14:9–11 (NKJV) lays out the consequences of that decision:

> Then a third angel followed them, saying with a loud voice, "If anyone worships the beast and his image, and receives his mark on his forehead or on his hand, he himself shall also drink of the wine of the wrath of God, which is poured out full strength into the cup of His indignation. He shall be tormented with fire and brimstone in the presence of the holy angels and in the presence of the Lamb. And the smoke of their torment ascends forever and ever; and they have no rest day or night, who worship the beast and his image, and whoever receives the mark of his name."

Yes, you will enjoy food, water, shelter and security for a brief time, but you will suffer the consequences for all eternity if you lose heart and take the mark of the Beast.

The following verse goes on to say, "Here is the patience of the saints; here are those who keep the commandments of God and the faith of Jesus" (Revelation 14:12 NKJV). The people of God will need patient endurance during this time of tremendous upheaval and suffering.

Before we get to that stage, we need to prepare our hearts and minds. The apostle Paul had suffered immensely to arrive at the place in his faith where he could say, "I can do all things through Christ who strengthens me" (Philippians 4:13 NKJV). He had already endured shipwrecks, beatings, imprisonment, starvation, humiliation and even death or near-death by stoning (after which Acts 14:20 says he "got up"). He knew by experience that Christ was all he needed to endure trials and tribulations.

As Bible prophecies continue to unfold, some will try to stay out of the fight and declare themselves neutral bystanders. But we warriors will need the courage available to us through the power of the Holy Spirit to take a stand for Christ.

### Courage to Shelter in God

In chapter 6 we discussed one of the stages in the end-times scenario, "the beast coming out of the sea" described in Revelation 13:1–8. We believe this involves the collapse of the world order, the failure of economic markets, and the rise of world leaders who will offer solutions to the global chaos.

As the Beast, the Antichrist, is "given authority over every tribe, people, language and nation" (Revelation 13:7), notice that there will be few places to hide and no place to remain neutral. It seems incredible but true that

the whole world was filled with wonder and followed the beast. People worshiped the dragon because he had given authority to the beast, and they also worshiped the beast. . . .

verses 3–4

Nobody knows when Christ will come back to "rapture" believers. The Church has lived through and is living through some horrific events. Being prepared for anything, at any time, is the word of the day. Jesus said it best (of course) in John 15:18–21:

> "If the world hates you, keep in mind that it hated me first. If you belonged to the world, it would love you as its own. As it is, you do not belong to the world, but I have chosen you out of the world. That is why the world hates you. Remember what I told you: 'A servant is not greater than his master.' If they persecuted me, they will persecute you also. If they obeyed my teaching, they will obey yours also. They will treat you this way because of my name, for they do not know the one who sent me."

For several centuries, the Church in many nations has enjoyed gracious standing and social status in society. Many towns and cities have a church or churches at their center. This has changed and is changing as you read this book. The rise of instant communication, internet, travel, public education, prosperity, leisure and a host of other factors have contributed to the decline of the Church in recent decades, including the closure of many churches during the COVID-19 pandemic.

Even now, before the time of the end, our friend retired U.S. Army Major General Robert Dees admits that "life is pretty tough for many people." He suggests what we need:

> It comes and goes, but we all get body-slammed at various times, so even now it's only common sense to get ready for the storms of life and learning how to best respond, hiding under the shelter of God's wings until the destruction passes. After that it's bouncing back and not getting stuck in toxic emotions like false guilt, anger and bitterness, but

getting better, wiser and stronger through adversity, so we can be ready for the *next* storm of life. That's what I call the resilience life cycle.[7]

## Courage to Fight

In developing courage and resiliency, we need to understand the fundamentals of spiritual warfare in order to fight the good fight. Paul says in 2 Corinthians 10:4 (NKJV) that "the weapons of our warfare are not carnal but mighty in God for pulling down strongholds." What are those weapons and how do we use them?

The weapons of our warfare are listed in Ephesians 6:14–17: the belt of truth, the breastplate of righteousness, the shield of faith, the helmet of salvation, the shoes of the Gospel and the sword of the Spirit. We will look at these weapons again in chapter 14, and others as well. But they will not do you much good if you don't know how to use them properly or train with them every day. One thing is clear: We develop courage by the constant use of these weapons.

Historical studies found that most of the soldiers who hit the beaches of Normandy, France, on D-Day did not fire a shot because of a lack of preparedness. Military historian S. L. A. Marshall, based on interviews he did with soldiers during World War II, estimated that no more than twenty percent, and generally as few as fifteen percent, had ever fired their weapons at an enemy.[8]

God has provided us with array of spiritual weapons to achieve victory in the last days, but like soldiers who never fire their guns, our spiritual weapons do little good unless we use them to engage the enemy.

In addition to the six weapons listed in Ephesians 6, people often miss the seventh weapon, the most powerful of them all—praying in the Spirit. This is Paul's encouragement on how to use this weapon effectively: "Pray in the Spirit on all occasions with all kinds of prayers and requests" (verse 18). Prayer is the most powerful weapon because it is the fuel that supplies the power to your arsenal.

Here are characteristics of courage taken from an Army evaluation form for a non-commissioned officer (NCO):

## THE NCO WITH COURAGE

* Calls it like it is. Ensures standards remain high In Accordance with (IAW) Army Regulations.
* Rejects status quo answers that may not paint the whole picture; instead provides fact-based information freely.
* Has unshakable will and dedication; materializes Army values with his or her actions.
* Is determined and loyal; stands behind beliefs.
* Has the courage to state the truth and the patience to present views logically.
* Stands firmly on convictions.

## THE BELIEVER WITH COURAGE

* Calls it like it is, according to and standing on the Word of God.
* Rejects status quo answers from the world in the end times; provides fact-based information from the Word of God.
* Has unshakable will and dedication; pleases God in the way he or she lives.

* Is determined and loyal. Stands behind his or her beliefs.
* Has the courage to state the truth and the patience to present views logically.
* Stands firmly on convictions.

## STRATEGIC SPIRITUAL EXERCISES

Here are some practical takeaways for unleashing last days courage in your life:

1. Identify things, places or situations that make you truly afraid.
2. Find Scriptures that help you understand and gain courage to overcome these fears. Some examples are Joshua 1, Ephesians 6:10 and Deuteronomy 6:10.
3. Remember the last time you won in your battle with fear. How did you do it?
4. Read biographies of believers who conquered fears in their lives.
5. Begin to face your fears by starting with the small ones first and building up to your bigger fears.

# CHECKLISTS

"For truly I tell you, until heaven and earth disappear, not the smallest letter, not the least stroke of a pen, will by any means disappear from the Law until everything is accomplished."

—Matthew 5:18

UPON PROMOTION to lieutenant colonel, I was assigned to the Pentagon in Washington, D.C., as the assignments officer for the chief of chaplains, responsible for placing 1,700 U.S. Army chaplains in their respective places of duty worldwide. This task was incredibly complex and difficult. Sometimes there were more than five hundred assignments to make in just a week.

But I had many highly intelligent chaplains working with me at various Army headquarters around the world who proved a great team, providing me with much needed input. I met with my leaders every six months at a conference during which we made the upcoming chaplain assignments. Our team huddled and came up with a list of more than thirty different factors to help us decide. These factors included things like how long the chaplain had been at the most recent station, last tour of duty, rank, promotability, any additional education needed, and so on.

It was a daunting task; in fact, it was overwhelming. Many people have asked me over the years how I got through this difficult process and survived. Of course, God helped me, as did my other team leaders and predecessors.

But the secret to my success was the checklist. I would not have survived without it. It started out on paper and ended up on my computer. These detailed checklists consisted of what I learned about the numerous assignments, listing what I needed to do to create a first-rate assignment process. Eventually, I used those checklists as the basis for future assignment conferences.

I had learned firsthand, during a six-month tour of Honduras, that checklists were an important part of the military. I was flying around the country on a Black Hawk helicopter to visit soldiers when I noticed the pilots consulting documents in their hands. Speaking to them on a headset, I asked what they were.

The co-pilot looked back at me with a smile. "Chaplain, we fly VFR [Visual Flight Rules] here, and not by navigational beacons, so we have to check everything by hand, including flying by maps and using checklists."

"Maps, too?" I asked.

"Yeah, we follow roads and rivers visually to navigate where we're going."

So I learned from those guys who relied heavily on their handheld maps and checklists. Our brains have only so much memory and bandwidth. Checklists free up some of your cerebral capacity consumed by the details of life, helping you to focus on more significant things. They help you avoid costly mistakes. And they simplify the process of outsourcing specific tasks.

For these reasons, the checklist needs to be among your most essential tools of life. In his book *The Checklist Manifesto,* author Atul Gawande calls to our attention that "checklists . . . remind us of the minimum necessary steps and make them explicit. They not only offer the possibility of verification but also instill a kind of discipline of higher performance."[1]

## Pre-Combat Checklists

One of the most important military checklists is the pre-combat checklist. It itemizes what a soldier needs to take into combat—weapon, ammunition, cleaning kit for the weapon, sleeping bag, personal hygiene and medical kits, clothing, combat boots, helmet, night-vision goggles, radio and other items.

AskTOP.net, a blog that connects people to a network of military leaders who answer Army leadership questions, notes the following about pre-combat checklists:

> When your Soldiers are preparing for a mission of any type, you must be certain that everyone is ready and everything is in order. If a weapon isn't working, if a radio's batteries are dead, if you don't have enough water or rations, the success of your mission and the safety of your platoon are threatened. As a platoon leader, it will be your job, and that of your NCOs, to ensure that your Soldiers have all the necessary clothing and equipment, that the equipment is in working order, that sanitary conditions are met, and that the platoon can operate effectively when called on. You do this through pre-combat checks and inspections."[2]

The pre-combat checklist is important for at least two reasons. First, you take only what you need into combat. And second, using the list significantly increases your odds of survival.

People in the military know the importance of having the right gear when it is needed most. The B-17, one of World War II's strategic bombers and one of the most important weapons the Allies possessed, highlights the importance of checklists.

During the 1930s, a competition was scheduled to determine who could produce the next wave of bombers for the United States—not with two engines but with four, as specified by the government. Boeing planned to demonstrate the flying capabilities of the B-17, also known as the Flying Fortress. But at the competition, in front of leaders of the Army Air Corps, it stalled on takeoff and crashed, killing the pilots. Boeing nearly lost the contract, and the company's existence hung in the balance.

During a think tank session, someone decided that pilots needed a checklist to fly this complex aircraft. So the B-17 became the first combat aircraft required to have a checklist as part of its takeoff and landing procedures.[3] According to Angle of Attack, a flight simulator company:

> By implementing the checklists, they flew 1.8 million hours with 18 B-17s without incident, proved to the government they were safe, and eventually nearly 13,000 were built. What is more telling is the images of these four engined, resilient monsters fending off the evil forces of the Axis Powers. And to think that this aircraft could have been eliminated from its place in history because they continued not to use checklists.[4]

## Biblical Checklists

Just as the checklist turned out to be key in helping the Allies win World War II, end-times warriors of God are wise to use checklists as prophetic events continue to speed up and we move closer to the time of Jesus Christ's return.

The Bible contains countless checklists that are the foundations of our spiritual heritage. Many serve as spiritual barometers. Consider the following.

### The Ten Commandments

1. You shall have no other gods before Me.
2. You shall make no idols.
3. You shall not take the name of the Lord your God in vain.
4. Keep the Sabbath day holy.
5. Honor your father and your mother.
6. You shall not murder.
7. You shall not commit adultery.
8. You shall not steal.
9. You shall not bear false witness against your neighbor.
10. You shall not covet.

How do the Ten Commandments (see Exodus 20:3–17) work as a checklist? Simple. They are an inventory of what things are important to us.

Take the first commandment: "You shall have no other gods before Me." Is there any priority higher in your life than God? Perhaps you will realize that work, sports, entertainment or something else rank higher on your list. Are those gods really that important or necessary?

Professional wrestler and actor Hulk Hogan created a post on Instagram during the coronavirus pandemic in 2020 that went viral, capturing the zeitgeist of that crisis.

In three short months, just like He did with the plagues of Egypt, God has taken away everything we worship. God said,

"You want to worship athletes, I will shut down the stadiums. You want to worship musicians, I will shut down Civic Centers. You want to worship actors, I will shut down theaters. You want to worship money, I will shut down the economy and collapse the stock market. You don't want to go to church and worship Me, I will make it where you can't go to church.

"If my people who are called by my name will humble themselves and pray and seek my face and turn from their wicked ways, then I will hear from heaven and will forgive their sin and will heal their land."[5]

## The Tabernacle

Moses received precise instructions in Numbers 26 on how to build the Tabernacle in the desert so the Israelites could worship God properly. These instructions were so detailed that they go on for many chapters in the Bible. God is a God of precision and clarity.

Don't think for one minute that Moses and his workers did not have a checklist of all the things necessary to build the Tabernacle. After all, Hebrews 8:5 says that the Tabernacle was "a copy and shadow of what is in heaven," an earthly replica of the heavenly version, which is one reason God warned Moses to "make everything according to the pattern shown you on the mountain."

## The Ark

In the life of Noah, we see a similar pattern of instructions and checklists. In Genesis 6:14–16 God gave Noah the following instructions before the flood:

"Make yourself an ark of cypress wood; make rooms in it and coat it with pitch inside and out. This is how you are to build it: The ark is to be three hundred cubits long, fifty cubits wide and thirty cubits high. Make a roof for it, leaving below the roof an opening one cubit high all around. Put a door in the side of the ark and make lower, middle and upper decks."

Not a lot of detailed instructions here, but Noah took what God told him and created a set of blueprints and detailed checklists so nothing would be forgotten or overlooked.

### Fighting Battles

David learned how to be a great warrior from the little things he had done every day. (Tending sheep in the rugged Middle East was no easy task.) Notice that he always asked for instructions from the Lord before battle. 2 Samuel 5:23–25 reveals the Lord's detailed instructions to David:

> "Do not go straight up, but circle around behind them and attack them in front of the poplar trees. As soon as you hear the sound of marching in the tops of the poplar trees, move quickly, because that will mean the LORD has gone out in front of you to strike the Philistine army." So David did as the LORD commanded him, and he struck down the Philistines all the way from Gibeon to Gezer.

## Following God's Orders

In these Scriptures, an important pattern emerges that we must understand as warriors of God in the last days. Notice in each of the preceding narratives that God spoke and his followers (Moses, Noah, David) obeyed.

It is no different in the New Testament with Jesus and His followers—and it is no different for us today. To know what God intends, we must listen to His instructions. He speaks to our hearts, through His Word, through circumstances, and oftentimes through other people. Checklists are simply a tool to ensure that we don't forget or overlook anything.

Our friend Sid Roth, host of *It's Supernatural!*, broadcast on Christian television networks around the world, says it is "hugely important" to listen to the Lord's instructions today. "We're about ready to enter the greatest move of God's Spirit in history," he says, "and shortly after that some real serious problems start. Obviously these are life-and-death matters."

It is so vital to follow God's orders, says Roth, that unless believers are ready, "we are not going to win, and our Bible says we're going to win. Historically, every time the Church gets dry and devoid of power, God sends His Spirit. So if there is not a move of His Spirit, I don't see the current generation standing a chance."

Since the devil controls much of our political and educational systems, as well as the media and Hollywood, Roth does not "see any chance for this current generation, short of a move of God's Spirit." For decades, perhaps longer, millions of people have been asking God to pour out His Spirit on all people, as described in Acts 2:17, which Roth believes is beginning to happen. And he cites the vision of Smith Wigglesworth, famous twentieth-century British evangelist, whose ministry demonstrated the miracles of Jesus. In Wigglesworth's vision he foresaw the "last great move of God's glory," says Roth, "and I happen to believe that this was from God, and I happen to believe it's already started on planet earth."

Wigglesworth saw an "outpouring of revival," Roth says, in which God performed many different types of miracles through "average people." Roth continues:

I've given it a name to distinguish it from other names—the greater glory of God. I see the greater glory of God doing nothing but increasing, not leaving like in the previous moves of God's Spirit—doing nothing but increasing until the return of Jesus. I further see this happening before we have prophesied end-times events, although they are in transition right now, too. . . . I see whole football stadiums packed with Christians and nonbelievers, especially young people . . . young college students who don't know their left hand from their right hand. They're into drugs and sex and pornography and blatant atheism—and I see them coming in, many of them sick, and walking out of those stadiums healed. I see them getting on their faces and repenting.[6]

## Checklists Do's and Don't's

Checklists should be written down and have a limited number of items—no more than ten. Also, it is important to memorize your list. Writing down your checklist is important, but having it in your heart is more important. It will become part of your daily routine.

Some people point out that checklists can lead to legalism, as if your salvation depends on what you accomplish and not on the grace of God. But we in the Church have veered so far into "freedom" and "grace" that we have largely ignored the disciplines of repentance, accountability, prayer, fasting, Bible reading and other spiritual masteries. A checklist is merely a reminder to do the important stuff.

The top priority on your warrior checklist should be spending time with God. Although it may seem a small and insignificant part of your day, you will quickly find that spending time with God via Bible study, meditation on the Word of God and prayer is the secret to walking in supernatural victory in the last days. In fact, there is no other higher priority.

Further, it is important to have both physical and spiritual checklists, given natural disasters and other emergencies, not to mention what the Bible tells us is coming. These checklists should include standard emergency provisions for you and your family—including food, water, shelter and other necessities—as well as security measures to protect your loved ones. Consult the appendix at the end of this book, "Army's Prioritized Checklist for the End Times," for more detailed information.

## End-Times Checklist

The following is a checklist of end-times events detailed in Scripture:

☐ *Global moral decay and ungodliness.*
There will be terrible times in the last days. People will be lovers of themselves, lovers of money, boastful, proud, abusive, disobedient to their parents, ungrateful, unholy, without love, unforgiving, slanderous, without self-control, brutal, not lovers of the good, treacherous, rash, conceited, lovers of pleasure rather than lovers of God—having a form of godliness but denying its power. Have nothing to do with such people.

2 Timothy 3:1–5

☐ *Rise of Iran and Turkey to dominate the Middle East.*
"In my vision at night I looked, and there before me were the four winds of heaven churning up the great sea. Four

great beasts, each different from the others, came up out of the sea. The first was like a lion, and it had the wings of an eagle. I watched until its wings were torn off and it was lifted from the ground so that it stood on two feet like a human being, and the mind of a human was given to it. And there before me was a second beast, which looked like a bear. It was raised up on one of its sides, and it had three ribs in its mouth between its teeth. It was told, 'Get up and eat your fill of flesh!'"

Daniel 7:2–5

☐ *Global economic and social chaos.*

When the Lamb opened the third seal, I heard the third living creature say, "Come!" I looked, and there before me was a black horse! Its rider was holding a pair of scales in his hand. Then I heard what sounded like a voice among the four living creatures, saying, "Two pounds of wheat for a day's wages, and six pounds of barley for a day's wages, and do not damage the oil and the wine!"

Revelation 6:5–6

☐ *Rise of the Antichrist.*

The beast was given a mouth to utter proud words and blasphemies and to exercise its authority for forty-two months. It opened its mouth to blaspheme God, and to slander his name and his dwelling place and those who live in heaven. It was given power to wage war against God's holy people and to conquer them. And it was given authority over every tribe, people, language and nation. All inhabitants of the earth will worship the beast—all whose names have not been written in the Lamb's book of life, the Lamb who was slain from the creation of the world.

Revelation 13:5–8

☐ *Rebirth of Israel in 1948.*

"Who has ever heard of such things? Who has ever seen things like this? Can a country be born in a day or a nation be brought forth in a moment? Yet no sooner is Zion in labor than she gives birth to her children."

Isaiah 66:8

☐ *Recapture of Jerusalem in 1967's Six-Day War.*

"They will fall by the sword and will be taken as prisoners to all the nations. Jerusalem will be trampled on by the Gentiles until the times of the Gentiles are fulfilled."

Luke 21:24

☐ *Rise of Babylon the Great.*

One of the seven angels who had the seven bowls came and said to me, "Come, I will show you the punishment of the great prostitute, who sits by many waters. With her the kings of the earth committed adultery, and the inhabitants of the earth were intoxicated with the wine of her adulteries." Then the angel carried me away in the Spirit into a wilderness. There I saw a woman sitting on a scarlet beast that was covered with blasphemous names and had seven heads and ten horns. The woman was dressed in purple and scarlet, and was glittering with gold, precious stones and pearls. She held a golden cup in her hand, filled with abominable things and the filth of her adulteries. The name written on her forehead was a mystery: BABYLON THE GREAT THE MOTHER OF PROSTITUTES AND OF THE ABOMINATIONS OF THE EARTH. I saw that the woman was drunk with the blood of God's holy people, the blood of those who bore testimony to Jesus.

Revelation 17:1–6

*Authors' note: Some Bible prophecy experts believe that the headquarters of the Antichrist, described in*

*Revelation 17–18, could be Neom, the futuristic city mentioned in chapter 1 now being developed in Saudi Arabia.*

☐ *Plans to build the third Temple.*

"So when you see standing in the holy place 'the abomination that causes desolation,' spoken of through the prophet Daniel—let the reader understand. . . ."

Matthew 24:15

*Authors' note: We believe this will happen in the middle of the seven-year period called the Tribulation, when the Antichrist will enter the rebuilt Temple in Jerusalem and proclaim himself to be God.*

☐ *Rise of globalism.*

[The beast] was given power to wage war against God's holy people and to conquer them. And it was given authority over every tribe, people, language and nation.

Revelation 13:7

☐ *Implantable microchips and similar devices.*

[The second beast] also forced all people, great and small, rich and poor, free and slave, to receive a mark on their right hands or on their foreheads, so that they could not buy or sell unless they had the mark, which is the name of the beast or the number of its name. This calls for wisdom. Let the person who has insight calculate the number of the beast, for it is the number of a man. That number is 666.

Revelation 13:16–18

*Authors' note: Artificial Intelligence (AI) and technology make the mark of the Beast possible for the first time in history.*

☐ *Popularity of transhumanism.*
"Just as it was in the days of Noah, so also will it be in the days of the Son of Man. People were eating, drinking, marrying and being given in marriage up to the day Noah entered the ark. Then the flood came and destroyed them all."

Luke 17:26–27

*Authors' note: We believe this refers to the rise of transhumanism in the lineage of the Nephilim, literally the "sons of God" (Genesis 6:4).*

☐ *Spread of apostasy.*
Don't let anyone deceive you in any way, for that day will not come until the rebellion occurs and the man of lawlessness is revealed, the man doomed to destruction.

2 Thessalonians 2:3

☐ *Worst persecution of Christians in history.*
"Then you will be handed over to be persecuted and put to death, and you will be hated by all nations because of me."

Matthew 24:9

☐ *Proliferation of weapons of mass destruction.*
"Therefore in one day her plagues will overtake her: death, mourning and famine. She will be consumed by fire, for mighty is the Lord God who judges her. When the kings of the earth who committed adultery with her and shared her luxury see the smoke of her burning, they will weep and mourn over her."

Revelation 18:8–9

☐ *Cataclysmic wars.*
"Nation will rise against nation, and kingdom against kingdom."

Matthew 24:7

## MILITARY CHECKLIST CATEGORIES

Following are some of the checklists used in the military:

* *Battle drills.* These are group skills designed to teach a unit to react and accomplish the mission in typical combat situations, including reacting to an ambush or chemical attack and evacuating wounded personnel from a vehicle.

* *Communications.* Checklists for how the military communicates in the field or in combat include operating a single-channel tactical radio in the field, antenna procedures, radio operating techniques, power sources and electronic warfare.

* *Convoy operations.* For these motorized operations, in which wheeled vehicles are the primary method of movement, checklists include vehicle maintenance and readiness, order of movement, medical evacuation procedures and reactions under enemy fire.

* *First aid.* Military medical aid checklists include individual soldiers' medical aid supplies, evaluating casualties and performing first aid for shock or bleeding.

* *Planning.* The primary tool for planning is the military decision-making process (MDMP). Checklists include identifying the problem, gathering information, analyzing the situation, developing options, evaluating alternatives, selecting an alternative solution and making the final decision.

## BELIEVER'S CHECKLIST CATEGORIES

* *Battle drills.* These checklists should include what is needed in order to fulfill God's will and direction in

your life. Examples include reacting to an enemy attack, preparing for God's new direction in your life and analyzing your current spiritual and well-being status.

* *Communications.* Checklists include instructions from God's Word on how to speak to and hear from God, improving interactions with your spouse and talking to nonbelievers. Communication can be vertical (to God) or horizontal (between people).

* *Convoy operations.* Checklists involve learning how to move in the will of God, following the leading of the Holy Spirit, transferring power from heaven and assisting spiritually wounded believers in crisis mode.

* *First aid.* These checklists including caring for believers wounded in church, uplifting saints who are struggling with addictions and applying prayer and the healing of the Holy Spirit to those in need.

* *Planning.* Compose checklists consisting of Scriptures that deal with making decisions (see the book of Proverbs, for example), learning to cope with difficult decisions, learning from wise mentors and discussing plans, goals and dreams.

## STRATEGIC SPIRITUAL EXERCISES

Here are some practical takeaways involving checklists:

1. Draft small checklists at first and build up to longer ones.
2. Determine to have several short, powerful lists that can help you get to the next level in your life.

3. Ask other strong leaders about their checklists.

4. Stick with it. Don't give up on your checklists even though you have not followed them in a while.

5. Ask the Holy Spirit for input into your lists.

PART 2

# BASIC TRAINING

# 9

# BOOT CAMP

Praise be to the LORD my Rock, who trains my hands for war, my fingers for battle.

—Psalm 144:1

*SUMMER 1986, Fort Dix, New Jersey, Chaplain Basic Course.* We have just finished a night "ruck march"—a forced march carrying heavy backpacks—and are being harassed and attacked by drill sergeants using riot control gas. As we stop in place, which gave me time to remove my helmet and get a breather, one of their grenade canisters lands in my helmet lying upside down on the ground.

The drill sergeants are prepping us to get ready. They assure us that the live ammunition being fired out of the machine guns is at least twelve to fourteen feet above our heads, but we get a stern warning: "Do not, under any circumstances, stand up!" The live machine gun fire is nearly nonstop, which means to me that more than one weapon is firing rounds above us.

I stay low, crawling under concertina wire in the night infiltration course, while drill sergeants keep barking out commands for us to keep our heads down. At the same time, simulation artillery is exploding all around us. Dirt sprays upward as I crawl forward. I have seen war movies like this; now I am living it. One question keeps being repeated in my mind: *Why did I volunteer to join the military?*

It is not the last time I question my decision. It is at times like this, when things get tough, that we question our motives, our calling and our sanity.

I have discovered through a series of hard times in training and in live combat what it takes to be a warrior of God. Here is what it takes: *the predetermined decision that you are not going to give up, no matter what.*

Yes, there will be times you question your sanity and even your faith. But if you are going to be a warrior for Jesus Christ, you will need the courage to break through the obstacles that stand in your way.

## Train as You Fight

In chapter 4 I mentioned the Army's maxim "Train as you fight." In other words, the conditions in basic training must be as close to combat reality as possible.

Basic training in the military is a regimented, multi-week ordeal that includes daily and sometimes hourly physical training, weapons qualifications, close-order marching, drills and ceremonies, military protocols, keeping a neat uniform, and similar disciplines. At the end of this chapter you will discover ten training principles to help prepare you for what is coming.

Just as the military puts soldiers through basic training to ready them for war, the end times requires spiritual warriors who are trained in the art of spiritual disciplines.

In biblical times (as we have seen), David learned many of the disciplines of training, such as protecting his sheep by fighting off bears and lions while shepherding flocks in the wilderness. He proved his mettle by killing Goliath with a stone in a sling, and learned many of his fighting skills in the army as King Saul's armor bearer and bodyguard.

David had to be skilled in the use of weapons, fighting techniques, taking orders, and other military disciplines. This training not only prepared him for combat but also helped him get into the minds of his enemies so he could defeat them. My U.S. Army chaplain friend Colonel Peter Brzezinski explains:

> If you understand the mindsets of those you are dealing with, whether in conflict or peace, you can go a long way to doing God's work and ministry. We learn lessons from great leaders God has raised up, like David. Imperfect as he was, he was a person of great military savvy, and the principles he used are still studied today in many arms of the military. For example, when you go to the armory school, or the infantry school, they talk about some of the tactics he used in biblical times.[1]

We learn by repetition and implementation. What we practice every day behind closed doors comes out in the heat of the battle. One of the reasons there is such widespread falling away from the faith today is that many people do not practice their faith moment by moment each day.

As a child, you were taught to tie your shoes. At first it seemed hard and it took a while to get the hang of it. Now you don't even think about it; it is automatic. It is the same with many things we do every day.

The reason we train as we fight is that when you are in the thick of combat, you react in the same way you have trained.

Repetition conditions you to perform without thinking. Warriors do not have the luxury of thinking when engaging the enemy. That is when training comes into play.

David acknowledged that God "trains my hands for war, my fingers for battle" (Psalm 144:1). In fact, my friend U.S. Army Chaplain (Lieutenant Colonel) Scott Koeman says that success on the battlefield for David and other Bible heroes boiled down to one quality:

> It's humility before the Lord, because every battle won was won by a king who had a humble heart. King Josiah was also a godly man, but he was filled with pride and didn't take wise advice—and in his own pride, he died in battle. So every time there is success in battle, it is because of humility before the Lord—every time without qualification. It is the Lord who wins the battle, and when we remain humble and let Him fight our fight, then we can be victorious.[2]

Just as God anointed David and other biblical heroes for victory in battle, He anoints and blesses His people throughout the week—not only preachers, but blue-collar workers, managers, CEOs, farmers and warriors to carry out divine assignments. Training begins when we acknowledge that we in ourselves can do nothing without Him (see John 15:5).

The apostle Paul wrote, "Everyone who competes in the games goes into strict training. They do it to get a crown that will not last, but we do it to get a crown that will last forever" (1 Corinthians 9:25). Joel Richardson says about this passage:

> Paul uses the analogy of Olympic athletes and compares that to the Christian life and to his life as an apostle. There is no question that the discipline necessary to be a soldier

carries a lot of lessons that most Christians today could learn from—prayer, devotion to the Lord, and more. All those things require discipline.[3]

## Training in the End Times

Some Bible scholars believe that Ezekiel 38–39 speaks of the end-times battle *before* Armageddon, but we believe these chapters speak of Armageddon itself, the last battle in history:

> "Son of man, this is what the Sovereign LORD says: Call out to every kind of bird and all the wild animals: 'Assemble and come together from all around to the sacrifice I am preparing for you, the great sacrifice on the mountains of Israel. There you will eat flesh and drink blood. You will eat the flesh of mighty men and drink the blood of the princes of the earth as if they were rams and lambs, goats and bulls— all of them fattened animals from Bashan. At the sacrifice I am preparing for you, you will eat fat till you are glutted and drink blood till you are drunk. At my table you will eat your fill of horses and riders, mighty men and soldiers of every kind,' declares the Sovereign LORD.
>
> Ezekiel 39:17–20

Notice the resemblance to this passage in Revelation that describes the final battle:

> And I saw an angel standing in the sun, who cried in a loud voice to all the birds flying in midair, "Come, gather together for the great supper of God, so that you may eat the flesh of kings, generals, and the mighty, of horses and their riders, and the flesh of all people, free and slave, great and small."
>
> Revelation 19:17–18

No, there are not two end-times battles; there is one. The Battle of Armageddon looms ever closer. Nation after nation is training its military for war.

Also notice that after the battle, God displays His glory, letting the world's nations know who the Lord is and why He has come:

> "Therefore this is what the Sovereign LORD says: I will now restore the fortunes of Jacob and will have compassion on all the people of Israel, and I will be zealous for my holy name. They will forget their shame and all the unfaithfulness they showed toward me when they lived in safety in their land with no one to make them afraid. When I have brought them back from the nations and have gathered them from the countries of their enemies, I will be proved holy through them in the sight of many nations. Then they will know that I am the LORD their God, for though I sent them into exile among the nations, I will gather them to their own land, not leaving any behind. I will no longer hide my face from them, for I will pour out my Spirit on the people of Israel, declares the Sovereign LORD."
>
> Ezekiel 39:25–29

The world around us trains for rewards that fade and applause that dissipates. Do you suppose Olympic athletes wait until a few weeks before the games to start training? Not on your life. They train for years—all for fading gold and money. Yet how many people remember the Olympic champions of just ten years ago?

So why are believers training? We are training for an eternal reward—that we may bring many into the Kingdom; reflect the glory of God to a lost and dying world; and receive, in the end, an eternal crown that will never tarnish.

## Learning the Basics

Followers of Christ must train in the spiritual disciplines that are present in the Word of God. We need to stay focused on what Scripture tells us to do. The Bible is our training manual. Paul summarizes it in 1 Timothy 4:7–10:

> Have nothing to do with godless myths and old wives' tales; rather, train yourself to be godly. For physical training is of some value, but godliness has value for all things, holding promise for both the present life and the life to come. This is a trustworthy saying that deserves full acceptance. That is why we labor and strive, because we have put our hope in the living God, who is the Savior of all people, and especially of those who believe.

Do you want to be a warrior for the Kingdom of God? Do you desire to be used in these final days to overcome evil and fight the good fight? Train yourself to be godly. Hear the passion in the apostle Paul's message to Timothy (above): "That is why we labor and strive, because we have put our hope in the living God, who is the Savior of all people, and especially of those who believe."

This is not legalism. It is seeking after God with everything you have. If you do not train for godliness, you will not reap the benefits.

How do we train? The list below reveals just a few spiritual disciplines, and how to approach each one. Start slowly with the right attitude of training for godliness, reaping the fruit and intensity of the Spirit, and preparing for the last days.

### Reading the Word of God Daily

Start your day with opening your Bible. If you are not already doing so, you will find many Bible reading apps for smartphones and plans on the internet that will help you. Find one that works for you. Don't worry how many chapters you read each day; focus on a few Scriptures and then apply them to your life, asking the Holy Spirit to lead you. Ask questions continually about what you have just read. Ask God to open "the eyes of your heart" (Ephesians 1:18). My wife and I read God's Word together every morning, then discuss its meaning and pray together. Powerful.

### Using Scripture as a Weapon

Just as Jesus in His temptation in the wilderness used Scripture as a weapon against Satan (see Matthew 4:1–11), so can you. The Bible contains thousands of promises, many of which we can use to arm ourselves for spiritual warfare. Paul explains: "The weapons we fight with are not the weapons of the world. On the contrary, they have divine power to demolish strongholds" (2 Corinthians 10:4). If obstacles, walls, closed doors and hindrances are blocking you, you will have to discern if it is a God thing or an attack or ambush from the enemy.

### Worship

The basic definition of worship is to attribute unto God His worthiness, and to bow down and pay reverence. Glorifying God and giving Him "a sacrifice of praise" (Hebrews 13:15) is not something to be done just on Sunday mornings; it is an attitude of the heart all week long, whether we feel like it or not. Learn to praise God during the day and in varying situations. Praise Him out loud and in your heart. Praise Him with uplifting music and in the quietness of silence. Use Scriptures, such as Psalm 145 (a psalm of David), to worship and praise Him. Pray, sing praises, magnify His name, raise holy hands, clap, dance before Him, and more. A choir went ahead of the army of Jehoshaphat, kind of Judah, to sing the praises of God and win the battle against a vast and mighty enemy army (see 2 Chronicles 20:21–24). Praise disperses and confuses our enemies and brings the power of God into dire situations. It unleashes God's power and brings into focus what is important—in the words of the Westminster Catechism, "to glorify God, and to enjoy him forever."

## Prayer

Kings of old inquired of the Lord before they went into battle. 1 Samuel 23:4 says King David often did this: "Once again David inquired of the LORD, and the LORD answered him, 'Go down to Keilah, for I am going to give the Philistines into your hand.'" We must adopt this mentality. Praying in the morning, praying the Scriptures, praying for others and praying for your needs are all good things. But we must be in touch with the Lord throughout the day, especially before big meetings, transitions, decisions, battles and other important events. To "inquire of the Lord" means to ask Him questions. God says in Jeremiah 33:3, "Call to Me, and I will answer you, and show you great and mighty things, which you do not know" (NKJV). He invites you to converse and commune with Him throughout the day. He invites you to talk to Him about helping others (interceding). You can even ask God about what you should pray about and how you should pray. Find a special place to get alone with Him and use that as your hiding place. The Pharisees had a habit of praying for public display so people would see them as pious and religious. That is the opposite of what Jesus told us to do: "When you pray, go into your room, close the door and pray to your Father, who is unseen. Then your Father, who sees what is done in secret, will reward you" (Matthew 6:6).

## Make Your Bed!

Foundational principles are the building blocks in becoming a warrior for God.

An example went viral that was given by retired U.S. Navy Admiral William H. McRaven, the former four-star commander of U.S. Special Operations Command at MacDill Air Force Base in Tampa, Florida. The former Navy SEAL credited with organizing Operation Neptune Spear, the special ops raid that led to the elimination of al-Qaeda leader Osama bin Laden, gave one of the best commencement speeches ever at his alma mater, the University of Texas at Austin, in 2014. "If you want to change the world," McRaven told the graduates, "start off by making your bed. . . . If you can't do the little things right, you will never do the big things right."[4]

What the admiral had learned in the Basic Underwater Demolition/SEAL (BUD/S) school, and what every soldier learns in basic training, is how to make your bed, and make it right, or you will pay the consequences and do push-ups. Why do you suppose the military puts such emphasis on making your bed? Order and discipline. Drill sergeants know that if soldiers can make their beds correctly, they will pay better attention to the details that might save their lives one day. Little things can turn into big things in a hurry.

So get the foundations of your life right. Start with your relationship with Christ. Is it real? Have you given your life over to the One who can save you from yourself and your sins? Start there. Then, if you start your day with God in prayer and reading His Word, you will receive inspiration, power and your orders for the day from your Creator.

Then get up and fix your bed!

Do little things like that matter to God? You bet they do. Look no farther than God's creation: "By faith we understand that the universe was formed at God's command, so that what is seen was not made out of what was visible" (Hebrews 11:3). God designed the universe and you in exquisite and excruciating detail, out of nothing—in the Latin, *ex nihilo*. Scientists are still trying to figure out how the universe runs and how it was designed.

Yet we have the mistaken belief that God is not about precision or accuracy, and that any old thing will do. Yes, God is a God of mercy, patience, love and understanding, but He is also a God of holiness and of order.

When we leave this planet and stand before the Creator of the universe, we will gaze upon the beauty, power, might and majesty of God for eons just to drink in the enormity of the scene. No wonder Isaiah cried out and fell before the Lord. Isaiah 6:1–5 gives us a glimpse:

> In the year that King Uzziah died, I saw the Lord, high and exalted, seated on a throne; and the train of his robe filled the temple. Above him were seraphim, each with six wings: With two wings they covered their faces, with two they covered their feet, and with two they were flying. And they were calling to one another: "Holy, holy, holy is the LORD Almighty; the whole earth is full of his glory." At the sound of their voices the doorposts and thresholds shook and the temple was filled with smoke. "Woe to me!" I cried. "I am ruined! For I am a man of unclean lips, and I live among a people of unclean lips, and my eyes have seen the King, the LORD Almighty."

How do we approach the unapproachable God? The writer of the book of Hebrews explained, "Without faith it is impossible to please God, because anyone who comes to him must believe that he exists and that he rewards those who earnestly seek him" (Hebrews 11:6).

The Greek word for *earnestly* in this verse is *ekzētousin*, which means to seek out, demand and inquire. Passion and intensity define this word. The true warrior is one who goes hard after God, passionately and diligently. The word best-selling author John Bevere uses is *relentless*—a continuous and passionate pursuit of God.

Of all the characters in the Bible, King David epitomizes this the best. He was a pursuer after God, a man after God's own heart. Read his passion in Psalm 63:1–5:

> You, God, are my God, earnestly I seek you; I thirst for you, my whole being longs for you, in a dry and parched land where there is no water. I have seen you in the sanctuary and beheld your power and your glory. Because your love is better than life, my lips will glorify you. I will praise you as long as I live, and in your name I will lift up my hands. I will be fully satisfied as with the richest of foods; with singing lips my mouth will praise you.

## MILITARY BASIC TRAINING PRINCIPLES[5]

The following are the Army's principles of basic training that will serve as a guide in your quest to become a noble and disciplined warrior of God:

* Commanders are responsible for training within their units.
* Non-commissioned officers (sergeants and above) receive guidance from their commanders and train individuals and small teams.
* Train as a "combined arms" (with infantry, artillery, engineers, armor and/or aviation, as needed) and "joint" team (with other military services).

* Train for combat proficiency in harsh, realistic conditions to emulate war.
* Train to the standards of the Army's Training and Doctrine Command.
* Train to adapt during combat as necessary.
* Train to maintain (fix) and sustain (supply).
* Learn to fight within the hierarchy: battalions, brigades, divisions and corps.
* Train to sustain proficiency.
* Train and develop leaders.

## BELIEVER'S BASIC TRAINING PRINCIPLES

* The Commander-in-Chief (the Lord) is responsible for training, but *you* are responsible before the Lord to receive and believe.
* Pastors, evangelists and Bible teachers are gifted to train believers.
* Train as a member of a group of believers called the Church.
* Focus your training on becoming a warrior of God.
* Train according to the standard: the Word of God.
* Be open at all times to the leading of the Spirit in your life.
* Commit to the long-term strategy of learning and growing in the Lord.
* Look toward growing in grace and going higher in your walk with God.
* Learn to be proficient in using the Word of God.
* Mentor younger believers, helping them grow in the grace of the Lord.

## STRATEGIC SPIRITUAL EXERCISES

Here are some practical takeaways from basic training to help you mature in your walk with the Lord:

1. Take a hard look at where you are spending your time during the day. What you do reflects who you are and what is important to you.
2. Discipline is a key word. Find out what that means in your life and how to grow in it.
3. Commit to both spiritual and physical exercise.
4. Read and study those who have mastered the basics in their lives.
5. Remember that doing something over and over, and expecting different results, is the definition of insanity.

# 10

# SPARTAN WARRIOR TRAINING

Physical training is of some value, but godliness has value for all things, holding promise for both the present life and the life to come.

—1 Timothy 4:8

*THE LIGHT FIGHTER COURSE, 7th Infantry Division, Fort Ord, California, summer 1987.* I was now a second lieutenant chaplain candidate reporting to the installation chaplain office at Fort Ord. The senior chaplain thought it would be a good idea to put me in the 7th Infantry Division's advanced course so I could experience what soldiers went through in preparing for combat.

I attended the briefing that outlined what we were about to experience. They assigned me to one of the infantry companies. Then we went to the field with nothing more than what we could carry on our backs (hence, the term *light fighter*).

Their motto was *Travel light, freeze at night.* I asked the senior NCO, a first sergeant, which vehicle was going to take us to our destination. He laughed and said, "We're taking a Mobile Personnel Carrier." I must have looked confused. Then he said, "Chaplain, look straight down at your boots, because that's what's taking you to the field today."

For two solid weeks I got to experience firsthand what was entailed in advanced infantry tactics, techniques and procedures—a team-carry of telephone poles; making Molotov cocktails and plastic explosives; night infiltration maneuvers; light infantry war-fighting skills; and much more. That training proved invaluable during future assignments in the war-torn countries of Iraq and Afghanistan.

Just to be clear, chaplains do not carry weapons in combat. At the time, however, I was a chaplain candidate, not a chaplain; I had not even graduated from seminary yet. (Things have changed significantly in the chaplain candidate program since then.)

I learned some unique lessons during that infantry training course. One of the most valuable lessons: In the military, as in life, you can accomplish little of real significance by yourself. I depended heavily on my team members to get through. That is the reason the Army assigns "battle buddies." A battle buddy is the person you are paired with during your basic training experience, ensuring that you learn that you need each other in combat to make it through. As I heard a hundred times in the Army, "There is no 'I' in team!" It does take a team—probably one of the reasons the Lord instituted the Church.

Who is my battle buddy? Pastor Claudio (Coco) Perez, pastor of Horizon Christian Fellowship in West Sacramento, California. Besides my wife, he is perhaps the single greatest influence in my life. We have been best friends for more than fifty years. He led me to the Lord and picked me up from my house each week and took me to church, Bible studies, conferences and conventions. We have been through a lot together, and I consider him one of the great Spartan warriors in the Kingdom of God.

Get a battle buddy! In these end times, when we will see the rise of extreme stress, pressure and instability worldwide, we need all the support we can get.

## Reasons for Spartan Training

Most people today recognize the term *Spartan*, but do you know what it means?

Sparta came to prominence around 650 BC as a city-state in ancient Greece. The focus and pride of Sparta was its army. The Spartan army was feared by all the surrounding nations because of the regimented training and discipline of its soldiers. Spartans normally fought to the death. It was considered treason if a Spartan surrendered.

Today the term *Spartan* is synonymous with hardship, discipline, severity and few comforts. The Spartan army is an example for warriors of God in the last days.

Jesus told His disciples, "In the world you will have tribulation; but be of good cheer, I have overcome the world" (John 16:33 NKJV). My friend retired U.S. Army Major General Robert Dees says of this passage: "Jesus said in this world we will have tribulation. It's not 'maybe'; it's 'will,' so let's get ready for it. We're all warriors, we get wounded, and we have to bounce back and fight again."[1]

That is a Spartan mindset!

The military has a saying: "Mission first. People always." What is our mission? Jesus told His disciples just before He ascended into heaven:

> "Go and make disciples of all nations, baptizing them in the name of the Father and of the Son and of the Holy Spirit, and

teaching them to obey everything I have commanded you. And surely I am with you always, to the very end of the age."

Matthew 28:19–20

My U.S. Army chaplain friend Colonel Peter Brzezinski explains that, as the end of the age draws near,

it's even more important that we do what is on the Lord's heart, which is to reach the lost with the Gospel and train the saints. Those two things are even more important today as we see the return of the Lord approaching, and as things degenerate in the world and evil gets more prominent, setting up the last battle. In the meantime, our task is the same: reach the lost and train the saints.[2]

These days we are experiencing events reminiscent of the book of Revelation, even if we scarcely realize what is happening. As Scripture unfolds, preparation must take priority over almost everything else—because the time is drawing closer.

Consider what happens in Revelation 8:7 (MEV) when the Lord begins striking the earth with His wrath:

The first angel sounded, and there followed hail and fire mixed with blood, and they were thrown upon the earth. A third of the trees and all the green grass were burned up.

The world witnessed wildfires in Australia recently that killed a "staggeringly huge" one billion animals. Meanwhile, California experienced its deadliest and most destructive fire season in 2018, with nearly 240 square miles burned, more than 18,000 structures destroyed, and the near incineration of the city of Paradise in the Sierra Nevada foothills.[3]

There are many theories about why so many fires are raging on our planet—climate change, mismanagement of the forests, changes in the earth's orbit and so on. But the severity of many of these fires has stunned the world.

Another similarity to Revelation—and another reason for Spartan training—comes from outer space:

> The third angel sounded, and a great star from heaven, burning like a torch, fell on a third of the rivers and on the springs of waters. The name of this star is Wormwood. A third of the waters became wormwood, and many men died from the waters, because they were made bitter.
>
> Revelation 8:10–11 (MEV)

Many scholars and students of prophecy believe the above passage indicates that the earth will be hit by an asteroid or meteor that will cause great death and destruction.

Currently the National Aeronautics and Space Administration (NASA) is tracking a "near-Earth asteroid called 99942 Apophis," 1,100 feet wide (the size of 3.6 football fields) due to approach earth on April 13, 2029.[4] This asteroid, if it hits the earth, would have the destructive force of 1,200 megatons (compared to the fifteen kilotons of the Little Boy atomic bomb dropped on Hiroshima, Japan, during World War II).[5] Apophis, named by NASA, is the Egyptian god of chaos and destruction. In Egyptian mythology Apophis is depicted as a giant snake.

NASA now downplays the threat, saying the odds of Apophis hitting earth are slim. But some scientists and other leaders are not as confident that this space rock traveling at 25,000 miles per hour will not strike our planet. An asteroid hit could kill millions of people, depending on its location. And there are many other NEOs (near-earth objects) that could pummel our world with devastating results. NEOs are so serious that NASA has a special office dedicated to studying and preventing major impacts.

A third reason for Spartan training is the upcoming threat to the economy. The following verses describe the financial situation on earth amid the opening of the seal judgments:

> When He opened the third seal, I heard the third living creature say, "Come!" I looked, and there was a black horse, and he who sat on it had a pair of scales in his hand. Then I heard a voice in the midst of the four living creatures saying, "A quart of wheat for a day's wages, and three quarts of barley for a day's wages, and do not harm the oil and the wine."
>
> Revelation 6:5–6 (MEV)

This is a reference to a coming shake-up of the world's economic system.

In good times most people are not as concerned about jobs or paying bills or keeping up with the mortgage. But as we were finishing this book, the coronavirus pandemic brought the global economy to a near standstill as more than half the planet was under stay-at-home orders. The International Monetary Fund issued a warning that the world was facing the "worst recession since the Great Depression."[6] Klaus Schwab, founder and executive chairman of the World Economic Forum, called for a "'Great Reset' of capitalism" to address the crisis.[7]

Government debt is another financial threat, ballooning in nations around the globe. It is a major problem that few are talking about, but it could be a key factor in the next economic collapse. If you look back in history, you see that no country can sustain large-scale borrowing against its future and survive.

We need an end-times mentality as things rachet up. We call it the Spartan spirit.

## The Spartan Spirit

The Spartan army is an example for warriors of God in the last days. As believers, we can follow the fighters of ancient Sparta as a model for training practices—which the Church calls "disciplines"—worthy of consideration for getting closer to God. We call these Spartan warrior training tools.

There were many practices the Spartans used that we would not consider today. But we can learn much from the spirit of Sparta—its rigorous advanced training. Brett and Kate McKay, in their article "The Spartan Way: The Mindset and Tactics of a Battle-Ready Warrior," write:

> The Spartans were an extremely reverent people. . . . Before embarking on a campaign, every morning while on it, and immediately preceding battle, oracles were consulted, sacrifices were made, and omens were examined. The sanction, or censure, of the gods was sought for every decision.[8]

What types of training did the Spartans undergo to maintain the famous Spartan military formation and achieve victory in battle? Principles of combat included the following:

- There is power in appearance. (Outward appearance reflects the inner warrior.)
- Always perform a pre-ritual battle. (Keep yourself disciplined before a fight.)
- Be both fierce and reverent. (Practice humility.)
- Endurance is the foundation of strength. (Be able to persevere in the heat of battle.)

- Speak (and think) laconically. (Make your enemy underestimate you.)
- Achieve mastery in your domain. (Be the best at what you do.)
- Fight from habit, not feeling. (Use your training.)
- Conquer or die. (Fight to the last man.)[9]

Let's explore the Spartan-like disciplines that warriors of God will need to survive and fulfill their destiny in the end times. The author of Hebrews states:

> Leaving the elementary principles of the doctrine of Christ, let us go on to maturity, not laying again a foundation of repentance from dead works and of faith toward God, of instruction about washings, the laying on of hands, the resurrection of the dead, and eternal judgment. This we will do if God permits.
>
> Hebrews 6:1–3 MEV

In other words, we need to move beyond the elementary things of God and move into advanced training to become more effective in our lives and ministries.

## Spartan Warrior Training Tools

Here are some training practices—what we call Spartan warrior training tools.

### Solitude

Sometimes we need to move away from the noise of life and get alone and quiet before God so we can hear His "still small voice" (1 Kings 19:12 NKJV). Noise—whether electronic gadgets, friends, phones, family, work or other intrusive things—is one of the weapons used against us in this restless world.

Solitude is time away from the noise that better positions you for quiet reflection about your life, journey and way of being. Solitude is not loneliness; it is being alone to spend time with God and yourself. Many of us are fearful of being alone. Try it and experience the awesome power of God's presence in a quiet place. Warriors need to get away from the battle.

We see this clearly in the story of Elijah after he defeated Baal on Mount Carmel and had 450 prophets of Baal killed. Queen Jezebel was furious and sought to destroy Elijah, who fled for his life. The story continues:

> Then [God] said, "Go out, and stand on the mountain before the Lord." And behold, the Lord passed by, and a great and strong wind tore into the mountains and broke the rocks in pieces before the Lord, but the Lord was not in the wind; and after the wind an earthquake, but the Lord was not in the earthquake; and after the earthquake a fire, but the Lord was not in the fire; and after the fire a still small voice.
>
> 1 Kings 19:11–13 NKJV

That is when Elijah experienced God—not in the powerful wind, strong earthquake or raging fire, but in that "still small voice," the whisper of God in a quiet place.

King David, while fleeing from his son Absalom, who was trying to kill him, experienced God in the wilderness of Judah: "O God, thou art my God, I seek thee, my soul thirsts for thee; my flesh faints for thee, as in a dry and weary land where no water is" (Psalm 63:1 RSV).

Jesus told His disciples to follow Him into a restful place for solitude: "Come with me by yourselves to a quiet place and get some rest" (Mark 6:31). The Lord knew He had to take time away from the ministry to renew and refresh not only Himself but also His disciples, who were ministering with him to the huge crowds.

Many times in my own ministry around the world to soldiers, families and civilians, I have needed time away from work and the crowds. My wife and I schedule time in places that are special to us, places in the great outdoors that provide a haven for solitude and reflection. This gives us a chance to pray alone and with each other, read spiritual books, and discuss what we hear God saying. (More about this in the next chapter, "Rest and Recuperation.")

### Fasting

The simple definition of fasting: going without, in order to focus on your relationship to God, so you may glorify Him. Most often it is abstaining from food, but it could be abstaining for a time from media (television, movies, sports, gaming, social media) or other distractions.

A poignant passage in the Bible about fasting is found in Daniel 10:2–6:

> At that time I, Daniel, mourned for three weeks. I ate no choice food; no meat or wine touched my lips; and I used no lotions at all until the three weeks were over. On the twenty-fourth day of the first month, as I was standing on the bank of the great river, the Tigris, I looked up and there before me was a man dressed in linen, with a belt of fine gold from Uphaz around his waist. His body was like topaz, his face like lightning, his eyes like flaming torches, his arms and legs like the gleam of burnished bronze, and his voice like the sound of a multitude.

Daniel had dedicated himself to get ahold of God for a specific period in order to understand God's purpose concerning his people. As Daniel did, he received an astounding vision of the angel Gabriel, who had been detained in battle for those three weeks with the prince of Persia. (We looked at that warfare in chapter 2.) Fasting had been the explosive power that created an opening for Daniel's prayers. God pulled back the curtain for him to see how things really were. He learned of the forces of God, His angels and battling in the unseen world against the forces of evil.

Fasting creates a way for us, too, to move closer to God and hear His whisper in that still, small voice. We need to understand and carry out the intentions of our Commander. Fasting is a helpful discipline as we seek God for His clarifying orders. Many times the answers to our petitions do not come right away. Like Daniel, we may experience roadblocks and obstacles without our even knowing it.

I have fasted many times over the years, especially when I needed to make an important, life-changing decision such as a career change or new direction in ministry. Fasting helps us focus on what is important—our relationship to God.

One such time occurred when I came up for promotion from major to lieutenant colonel. I needed to know whether God wanted me to stay in the Army or move into pastoral ministry. The answer came clearly one day when the board of the church with which I was connected decided to go another direction. I had my answer and have never regretted taking responsibility for the spiritual well-being of Army installations around the world.

### Sabbath Observance

At Camp Taji in Iraq, where I spent some time, there was a Forward Arming and Refueling Point (FARP). It was like a NASCAR pit crew, only for attack helicopters. FARP soldiers transfer hundreds of gallons of fuel and thousands of pounds of ammunition into aircraft to keep them in the fight and the enemy on their heels. An aircraft can land, be refueled and reloaded with ammunition, and get back into the air in a matter of minutes.

With war raging around us, it is important to understand the role of keeping the Sabbath. Church is our FARP—the filling station where we go to glorify God, bless His name corporately, get invigorated by His Word, pray, take Communion, enjoy fellowship with other believers, and go back out to touch a lost and dying world.

Many today take the church as a social club, a meeting place or a place of duty. It is not any of those things. Some view the Sabbath as a burden or a box to be checked on the holiness list. If going to church is burdensome and wearying to you, something is wrong—either your spiritual condition or the church you are attending. Take a hard look at both. If you ask God, He will give you discernment.

There is great misunderstanding about what the Sabbath is about. Why is Sabbath observance important for a spiritual warrior? And why is it so important to God as to be included as one of the Ten Commandments? Let's look at Exodus 20:8–11 (MEV):

> Remember the Sabbath day and keep it holy. Six days you shall labor and do all your work, but the seventh day is a Sabbath to the LORD your God. On it you shall not do any work, you, or your son, or your daughter, or your male servant, or your female servant, or your livestock, or your sojourner who is within your gates. For in six days the LORD made heaven and earth, the sea, and all that is in them, and rested on the seventh day. Therefore the LORD blessed the Sabbath day and made it holy.

Simply put, God instituted the Sabbath so we could spend one day resting from our labors to glorify and spend time with Him. Some people get caught up in whether we should observe the Sabbath on Saturdays or Sundays. The important thing is to set aside one day a week. (The early Christians used the first day of the week as their day to worship God.)

The Sabbath had its beginning in Genesis 2:2: "On the seventh day God completed His work which He had done, and He rested on the seventh day from all His work which He had done" (MEV).

Let's get something straight: God does not need to rest. Remember, "he who watches over Israel will neither slumber nor sleep" (Psalm 121:4). The actual word in Genesis used for rest is *Sabbath*, meaning to cease from labor. God could have created the world in one moment by the word of His mouth. He took seven days to show His care for creation, for our sakes. He used a process to enjoy the works of His hands so we might glorify Him in all things.

One scientist discovered recently that there are not billions of galaxies in the known universe, as once thought, but around two trillion galaxies, and each galaxy contains between one hundred to two hundred billion stars.[10] That is mind-bogglingly awesome! We get to glorify God each moment of every day, and especially on the Sabbath.

I like the word *pause* instead of *rest*. God paused from creating. Keeping the Sabbath is one of the Ten Commandments because God knew that His people would need to pause from or cease their regular work in order to focus on what is truly important—their relationship with Him.

Going aside to worship also brings God's perspective:

All day long I have been afflicted, and every morning brings new punishments. If I had spoken out like that, I would have betrayed your children. When I tried to understand all this, it troubled me deeply till I entered the sanctuary of God; then I understood their final destiny.

Psalm 73:14–17

The psalmist saw difficulty, distress and evil prospering until he entered the sanctuary and realized the "final destiny" of those who oppose God.

The Sabbath refreshes and renews our worldview, gives us strength for the fight, and renews our confidence in God. Take every chance you can to quiet yourself on the Lord's Day and be with His people in order to face the battles in front of you.

### Fellowship

We need each other for support, for building our faith, and for edification. Acts 2:42 sums it up this way: "They devoted themselves to the apostles' teaching and to fellowship, to the breaking of bread and to prayer." This is the finest example in the Bible to explain what fellowship is about. Just as the Father, Son and Holy Spirit have been in relationship and communion for eternity, the example is set for the rest of us to follow. Fellowship is all about community and sharing.

Being around others of like faith is where we draw our strength, endurance and support. Sharing in Bible studies, prayerful conversation and spiritual mentoring is the art and practice of fellowship.

One tactic of our enemy is to isolate us, to draw us away from other believers and to cut off fellowship. Many Christians today say they don't need to attend church or have fellowship with other believers. That is the individualism of Western thought. It is dangerous. As I said earlier, drill sergeants yell at the troops all the time, "There is no 'I' in team!" The military by nature is a team. No one goes into battle alone, and no one leaves a battle buddy alone on the field of combat.

There are many more disciplines and practices—including personal reflection, meditation, benevolence, service, simplicity and silence—to seek and practice. All are beneficial and good for the soul. And all help us to train and fight like Spartans.

## SPARTAN PRINCIPLES

* ⋆ There is power in appearance. (Outward appearance reflects the inner warrior.)
* ⋆ Always perform a pre-ritual battle. (Keep yourself disciplined before a fight.)
* ⋆ Be both fierce and reverent. (Practice humility.)
* ⋆ Endurance is the key to victory. (Be able to persevere in the heat of battle.)
* ⋆ Make your enemies underestimate you.
* ⋆ Be master of your domain. (Be the best at what you do.)
* ⋆ Fight from habit, not feeling. (Use your training.)
* ⋆ Conquer or die. (Fight to the last man.)

## BELIEVER'S SPARTAN PRINCIPLES

* ⋆ Reflect the glory of God inside you to the world.
* ⋆ Be constant in your devotions.

* Practice humility.
* Have the mindset of enduring to the end.
* Seek solitude with the Lord. Get alone with God for more power in your life.
* Fast not only from food but from other distractions in your life.
* Keep the Sabbath—not out of obligation, but of obedience and necessity.
* Fellowship with other believers for strength.

## STRATEGIC SPIRITUAL EXERCISES

Here are some practical takeaways for Spartan warrior training in the end times:

1. Purposely set aside time for being alone with God and yourself.
2. Try fasting from television, movies, news, sports, social media or something else for a week.
3. Seek times of fellowship with other believers.
4. Study Scriptures that help you nurture humility (see Colossians 3:12; James 4:6; the book of Ephesians) and ask God to help you carry out His divine purpose for your life.

# 11

# REST AND RECUPERATION

Because so many people were coming and going that they did not even have a chance to eat, [Jesus] said to them, "Come with me by yourselves to a quiet place and get some rest."

—Mark 6:31

MILITARY PROGRAMS incorporate rest and recuperation (R&R) into their operational orders in hostile environments or combat zones for a reason. The intensity of war, the stress of being away from home, the pressure of operating in an unpredictable and hostile environment, and unknown outcomes all add up very quickly to hamper a soldier's ability to stay focused on the mission.

This hostile environment (as we discussed in chapter 5) is aptly named VUCA: "volatility, uncertainty, complexity and ambiguity." This is exactly what a warrior in combat faces daily. So into military operations that stretch on for a year or more, smart military leaders embed an R&R program. This is to help soldiers get away from the VUCA environment and relax in a non-threatening, welcoming place. The military understands that a soldier cannot survive in a hostile environment for an entire year. You just won't make it, mentally or emotionally, so they take you out for R&R.

Soldiers fighting in a combat zone need a reason to keep fighting and putting their lives on the line. If they can say to themselves that they will be in an R&R zone in a few weeks or months, not having to worry about the stress of combat, it acts as a carrot for them to think, *There are things up ahead that I'm really going to enjoy. I can stick it out right now because the clock is ticking and I'll be there soon.*

You may not live in a combat zone, but you, too, need periodic R&R to get away from it all. There are times we just need to get away from the hustle and bustle, so we go on vacations, to retreats and places where the environment is less stressful. During those times we get to rest, unwind and recuperate.

Jesus understood the importance of R&R. He told His disciples to go with Him "to a quiet place and get some rest" (Mark 6:31). Since they were often around crowds, there were times they needed to rest and prepare for the next leg of their ministry.

Warriors of God, even amid the demands of our careers, ministries and families, also need time to regain focus, sensibility and equilibrium, because we just cannot keep fighting and fighting. It is the same with pastors. Without R&R they can burn out or be ineffective in their callings; so there are times they must pull back from the front lines of spiritual warfare.

In many respects, life stressors and spiritual warfare are similar. We can easily become casualties in this war. Our enemy would like to use the daily grind to wear us into the ground. No, bullets are not flying overhead, and combat is much more intense and demanding than daily living. But rest in our culture is almost a forgotten term, especially during this age of distraction. We are so connected to our smartphones, schedules and appointments that, for many of us, there is no time to rest—or so we tell ourselves. In fact, some of us pride ourselves on being busy. A sign of success is a full schedule and a packed calendar. But distraction without purpose is one of the surest signs of a person needing renewal and rest.

We see the consequences of this with pastors who burn out because they are so busy doing God's work that they do not take care of themselves. In a recent LifeWay Research poll of 1,500 pastors, 54 percent found the role of pastor "frequently overwhelming"; 53 percent were "often concerned about their family's financial security"; and 48 percent saw the demands of ministry as "more than they can handle."[1] Military chaplains and soldiers experience the same thing, which is why the military requires rest and recuperation.

For pastors, chaplains, soldiers and civilians—people from all walks of life—there comes a point when, not rested and not taking care of your physical, psychological and spiritual needs, you become ineffective. We saw in the last chapter that God created the Sabbath as a day of rest once a week, but many people today do not heed the Fourth Commandment. Warriors need rest. Without it they become ineffective in combat.

Rest, like most things, does not just jump onto your schedule. Corporate leaders, first responders, pastors, ministers, evangelists, missionaries, mothers, fathers, caretakers and ordinary foot soldiers need to plan for rest on a regular basis.

## Lessons from the Cave of Adullam

A story in the Old Testament exemplifies why warriors of God need R&R from time to time. David was hiding from

King Saul in the cave of Adullam because Saul was trying to kill him. The prophet Samuel had foretold the end of Saul's reign, and had anointed David as king, but Saul would not submit to the will of the Lord and sent his men in search of David to kill him. For four years David was on the lam, hiding with his men in shelters, strongholds and caves. For example:

> David departed from there and escaped to the cave of Adullam. And when his brothers and all his father's house heard it, they went down to him there. There gathered to him every one that was in distress, and every one in debt, and every one that was discontented. So he became captain over them. Now there were with him about four hundred men.
>
> 1 Samuel 22:1–2 MEV

Archaeologists and historians tell us that Adullam was one of the royal cities of the Canaanites located on the old Roman road in the Valley of Elah, the place of David's extraordinary victory over Goliath. It was one of the towns that King Rehoboam, grandson of King David, later fortified against Egypt.[2]

The cave of Adullam has been determined to be about two miles from where the battle with Goliath took place and about thirteen miles west of Bethlehem. Near this site is a peak about five hundred feet high punctuated with numerous caverns. David gathered in one of these caves with his men who were "in distress" or "in debt" or "discontented."

As we become battle ready and battle focused, there are some lessons from the cave of Adullam that we can apply to our lives today. As David and his band of brothers huddled together, they had time to reflect, plan and envision a new chapter in their lives. As they looked out over the valley below, they could sense new vistas and accomplishments that had never crossed their minds before.

If we want to be battle ready and rebuild that which has been lost in our lives, we need to get alone with God and become invigorated with the fresh wind of His Spirit. David faced ongoing persecution from Saul by regrouping, recalculating and reigniting his faith in the God who had defeated the giant not far from where he was now hiding. Sometimes we need a new start, away from the pace and crowds.

Also, David did not go it alone. He drew like-minded individuals who, as it turned out, would fight to the death for him. Those who are truly depressed do not want anyone around—just the opposite of what they need! We all need support—like-minded people full of faith to encourage us to stay on the path to victory.

Author and filmmaker Joel Richardson says:

> I believe the Church today could learn much from King David, who trusted in God, and as a result was fearless. He didn't live by fear. He didn't live by anxiety, but was willing to take on giants. I'm looking right now and saying, Where are the Davids of this generation who will rise up and confront the Goliaths of our time because they have confidence in the Lord? They are not afraid of losing their own lives. They are not afraid of losing anything, because they trust that the battle belongs to the Lord.[3]

### Repurposing

I had an experience like King David's in Saudi Arabia right after Desert Storm in the spring of 1991. My unit, the 43rd Air Defense Artillery Regiment that uses Patriot missile systems, was deployed to protect airfields and oil refineries. My unit was designed to shoot down enemy combat planes and missiles.

Early one morning the Bravo battery commander rushed into my quarters at Khobar Towers in Dhahran, Saudi Arabia. "Chaplain," he exclaimed, "get to the bunker now. We have an inbound Scud to our location."

The Patriot radar had detected a Scud—an Iraqi surface-to-surface missile with a large explosive payload—that had been launched out of Iraq and was headed our way at that very moment. It was time to scramble to the nearby underground bunker, a large concrete shelter that you entered by stairwell. I got down there in a hurry.

When I arrived, many soldiers were already there. You could have heard a pin drop in the bunker because of the tension. Everyone was in deep thought. In those few minutes (which seemed like an eternity), I had time to reflect on the important things in life. I prayed silently for our troops and the situation we were in.

The Scud did not hit our location. But in that bunker—my own cave of Adullam—I found the opportunity to reprioritize and repurpose my life for the glory of God. I realized that we are all but a hairsbreadth away from eternity at any moment. I purposed to walk closer to the Lord, hold deep my relationships with family and friends, and ensure that everyone around me heard about Jesus Christ, the only true center of my life.

Is it time for you as God's warrior to refocus and repurpose, too?

### Rising Up

Dr. Robert Mawire, founder and president of WRNO Worldwide—a global broadcasting platform out of Fort Worth, Texas, with the third-largest reach among shortwave radio networks, after Voice of America and the BBC—says the end times could be the Church's finest hour as God pours out His Spirit on the world (see Joel 2:28 and Acts 2:17–21):

> I believe that when the Spirit of God comes upon the Church, we're going to be a triumphant, victorious Church. Jesus is not coming back for a defeated Church in fear and hiding. No, it's going to be the most glorious time. Our God is bigger than external circumstances. Revelation 3:10 says, "I also will keep you from the hour of testing" [NASB]. Not "take you away" but "keep you from." In other words, it's going to be a larger multiplication of food and angels on assignment; it's going to be like Egypt. While the rest of Egypt was being tried, God was blessing His people.

Mawire says that what the devil does in the end times, and what the world does, is the "sideshow." He goes on to explain:

> The real show is the anointing coming upon the Church, the vindication of the Church, the rising up of the Church to be a militant, glorious Bride without spot or wrinkle. That's the exciting thing, the wondrous thing. In terms of what shall we eat, He said, "I'll give you all those things." You don't even have to ask because God's got total provision and there is nothing to worry about, but to get excited.[4]

John Ramirez, internationally known evangelist and former satanic cult (Santeria) high-ranking priest in New York City, says the Church needs to step out of the boat and understand that there is a spiritual war raging in the heavenlies, and that we are part of that war:

> We're more than conquerors. The remnant that God has today doesn't look like regular church. They're armed and dangerous out there, doing the work of God. They're doing

spiritual warfare—intercession. Pastors are setting people free. People are coming in with cancer and they go back to the doctors and there is no more cancer. They go to the doctor and there is no more diabetes. These are infirmity spirits that are being cast out.

People don't just want to hear preaching. They want to see the power of the demonstration of the Holy Spirit. Jesus came on the scene and preached, but He had power. Paul came on the scene and preached, but he had power. Peter came on the scene and preached, but his shadow healed people. He had power. The first three hundred years of the church had power. So what's going on today?[5]

## Enemy Strategies

British writer C. S. Lewis wrote the delightful and popular book *The Screwtape Letters* in 1942, filled with fictional correspondence between a senior devil, Screwtape, and a junior tempter named Wormwood. Screwtape reviews Wormwood's tactics, techniques and procedures in tempting a particular man. This imaginary riff by Erik Lokkesmoe, based on Screwtape's diabolical advice, describes one of many end-times strategies actually being employed against believers today:

> Good news! The latest commendations have arrived from the Council of the Pit. You impress the lower-downs, my zealous Wormwood. They have heard of your schemes on the Noise Proliferation Committee (NPC). Indeed, places of solitude and moments of silence grow ever more scarce in the Enemy's vast and vulgar dominion. Oh, what euphoria to see his insufferable creatures rush to fill the dead air with a cacophony of cell phones and [Muzak], leaf blowers and manipulated car exhaust pipes, 24-hour news and iPods. Those

nauseating humans cannot escape their self-made dungeon of din! My pride bubbles like brimstone, Wormwood.[6]

In this fanciful depiction, the very real plan by the enemy of our souls is distress and distraction, using the powerful weapon of noise. If he can keep us from hearing God's still, small voice, and communing with Him, then he has achieved a great victory over our lives.

I learned this in recent years when I moved from the city to the country. I sleep more deeply and soundly out in the country, where nature has an allure not found in fast-paced city life.

Not everyone, I realize, can move out of the city—hence the need for rest and retreat. As the time of the end approaches, there is a sense of things speeding up, whether in technology, entertainment, science or education. The amount of knowledge floods us with unlimited options, distractions and noise. The more we are immersed in it, the more time we need away from it.

Another end-times strategy is the advent of artificial intelligence (AI), which we now find at the heart of many technologies, including smart cars, autonomous drones, robotics, weapons of warfare, speech recognition, machine learning platforms, AI–optimized hardware decision management systems, deep learning platforms, and biometrics, to name a few. As with all new technologies, each has distinct advantages, but these new digitized tools are increasing our dependence on them.

The promise of more leisure time and less intrusion into our lives is a lie. With the rise of AI, we are finding new addictions to the internet, alarming intrusions into our psyches, and a host of other soul-numbing contrivances that we have yet to hear about.

The real strategy of the "god of this age" (2 Corinthians 4:4) is to control mankind through weaponized technologies that now cannot be stopped, even if we wanted to. The more time we are unplugged and away from these technologies, the better off we are.

## Rest and Recuperation in Scripture

Here are some Scriptures we find encouraging and comforting, promising R&R in the end times:

- Isaiah 40:28–31: "Do you not know? Have you not heard? The LORD is the everlasting God, the Creator of the ends of the earth. He will not grow tired or weary, and his understanding no one can fathom. He gives strength to the weary and increases the power of the weak. Even youths grow tired and weary, and young men stumble and fall; but those who hope in the LORD will renew their strength. They will soar on wings like eagles; they will run and not grow weary, they will walk and not be faint."
- Matthew 11:28–29: "Come to me, all you who are weary and burdened, and I will give you rest. Take my yoke upon you and learn from me, for I am gentle and humble in heart, and you will find rest for your souls."
- Psalm 127:1–2: "Unless the LORD builds the house, the builders labor in vain. Unless the LORD watches over the city, the guards stand watch in vain. In vain you rise early and stay up late, toiling for food to eat—for he grants sleep to those he loves."
- John 16:33: "I have told you these things, so that in me you may have peace. In this world you will have trouble. But take heart! I have overcome the world."

- Philippians 4:6–7: "Do not be anxious about anything, but in every situation, by prayer and petition, with thanksgiving, present your requests to God. And the peace of God, which transcends all understanding, will guard your hearts and your minds in Christ Jesus."

## MILITARY R&R

The Rest and Recuperation (R&R) program is an essential element of the military. These are some of its benefits:

* Respite from the stresses associated with combat missions during tours of duty.
* Allowing soldiers the ability to focus on family and friends when they return home.
* Helping reenergize and prepare service members and civilians mentally for the remainder of their tour.
* Improving mission performance and the well-being of the troops.

## BELIEVER'S R&R

End-times warriors of God also need rest and recuperation. Here are some suggestions:

* Get away from daily stresses to focus on your relationship with the Lord.
* Put R&R on the calendar for a location away from home in order to reflect deeply on the Lord and all that is truly important.

* Locate retreat centers that specialize in Christian wellness.
* Develop a deep and abiding relationship with those who are closest to you in Christ.

## STRATEGIC SPIRITUAL EXERCISES

Here are some practical takeaways for R&R:

1. Sit down and map out your next R&R location.
2. Avoid a guilt trap about spending time on your well-being.
3. Bring solid biblical reading materials with you, as well as enjoyable books.
4. Focus on areas of your life that need refueling and refitting.

# 12

# OBSTACLES, OBSTRUCTIONS AND OPPORTUNITIES

Everybody has a plan till they get punched in the mouth.

—Mike Tyson, former heavyweight boxing champion

"In the world you will have tribulation. But be of good cheer. I have overcome the world."

—John 16:33 MEV

*FALL 2005, NIGHTTIME, somewhere over Iraq.* I am strapped into a Sikorsky UH-60 Black Hawk flying fifty feet above the ground. I hitch rides whenever and wherever I can so I can be with our troops. Tonight we have a full complement of soldiers (eleven) in the helicopter with combat gear. This is the longest ride, and lowest to the ground, that I have been on up to this point in the war.

We are flying from southern Iraq to the northern part of the country. During this ride in the darkness, I am reminded that I could be down there on the ground in a convoy going through obstacles and obstructions. I have done that, so I am grateful to be flying. Flying has its own set of problems, but one thing we do not have to deal with is roadside obstacles, obstructions and improvised explosive devices (IEDs).

Then I remember that just a few weeks prior, I was in Afghanistan in a convoy to deliver much-needed clothes and items to the Pashtun tribes. Along the road were warning signs featuring skulls and crossbones, telling us not to get off the road due to minefields. I am glad I am not there tonight.

In Afghanistan, the U.N. Mine Action Service estimates that more than eighteen million "explosive remnants of war," or ERWs, including 737,000 Anti-personnel (AP) mines, have been "cleared" since 1989.[1] Tragically, 1,426 Afghan civilians were killed or injured by mines and ERWs in 2018 alone.

Just as landmines pose a grave danger to soldiers and civilians in Afghanistan and other war-torn regions, Christians also face obstacles and obstructions as we approach the end times. One of the biggest problems that plagues us today: We go to church on Sunday, get spiritually pumped up, go home, and then go back to work on Monday and lead lives disconnected from the Word of God until the following Sunday. Armed with only the spiritual training we receive on Sunday, we are left to face the obstacles and obstructions that life, work and the devil throw at us all week long.

This may work during times of prosperity and peace, but what about when times get harder and the second Great Depression hits or the Antichrist rises to power? How will the meager spiritual discipleship that most Christians get on Sundays—those of us who even go to church—help deal with those scenarios?

Evangelist John Ramirez describes one part of the scenario:

Secret societies are controlling the world, controlling the systems of the world, controlling systems in the demonic world. These secret societies are establishing the groundwork of the enemy through music, media, politics, movies. It's all part of the devil's playbook. It's all coming together—a one-world order and one-world religion. It's being played out in the media, in the hate and division, cultures against cultures, generations against generations. The secret societies are re-grouping, and after they come out of the locker room, so to speak, they're going to bring the game to the world. The deception is going to be so great that Jesus said that, in the last days, even the elect could be fooled. So they're setting up the stage for the Antichrist.[2]

Dr. Mawire, founder of the WRNO Worldwide short-wave radio network, believes that the "Antichrist is alive and well today." He also believes, based on his interpretation of the timeline in Daniel 12 and Revelation 11, that a "major, major event will reveal the Antichrist to the world."[3]

Meanwhile, plans are being made to the build the third Temple in Israel. "I met with the head of the Sanhedrin," says Mawire, "and he's ready now. Religious courts are being set up. I've been in one of them. Everything they need for that building has already begun. They've been given the right to Jerusalem and they now have the opportunity to build their third Temple."

More than one hundred Scriptures predict the rise of the Antichrist, including 2 Thessalonians 2:4, which says that the ruler of a coming world government will "[set] himself up in God's temple, proclaiming himself to be God."[4] Will we be prepared for such an event?

## "Step on It!"

In chapter 8 we saw that soldiers in basic training get a dose of what real combat is like. By experiencing realistic training, troops are prepared for future wars. In other words, obstacles are good for soldiers and may, in fact, help save their lives in combat.

In the early 1990s, I was stationed at the Joint Multinational Readiness Center in Hohenfels, Germany. My tank unit, the 37th Armor Regiment, was in the middle of intense combat training, using the multiple integrated laser engagement system (MILES). It is a very sophisticated system that uses laser transmitters to simulate combat conditions. Think laser tag on steroids. Every soldier and vehicle was fitted with transmitters, so that each "hit" with a simulated round was indicated by a flashing light.

The "observer controllers" (OCs) had "god guns" that they could use to "kill" you or "disable" an armored vehicle. These OCs had the power to point their god guns at you and kill you and your vehicle so that you were no longer part of the battle. If they pointed their weapon at you, it would trip a yellow flashing light on your MILES-equipped vehicle, and you were dead in the water.

My chaplain assistant and I were in our Humvee when I received a call from the commander telling me to get to the site of a real-world accident immediately. Two Bradley Fighting Vehicles (an armored infantry transport vehicle with a high-powered cannon) had rolled over, and the accident involved injuries. They needed prayer and help. So I said to my assistant, "Step on it. We've got to get to that accident site right now."

"Sir," he protested, "we can't possibly get through all the roadside obstacles and obstructions, let alone that there are OCs, soldiers and vehicles in the middle of training right now."

But the need might be pressing.

"I don't care what you have to do," I replied. "Get there."

What happened next is the stuff of movies.

I said a quick prayer, my assistant floored that Humvee, and we took off like a bat out of the abyss. We plowed right through the middle of a crossroad full of simulated landmines, barbed wire, tanks, Bradleys and a bunch of OCs shooting their god guns at us and yelling at us to stop.

I really wish I had a video of that scene. My assistant did some brilliant driving around the obstacles, obstructions and everything preventing us from getting to our intended destination. That battlefield had all kinds of obstacles, obstructions, simulated minefields, armored vehicles and—worst of all—those OCs with their "god guns."

But we arrived in record time, albeit a little stressed from our harried adventure, charging through the middle of simulated combat. Once we got to the accident scene, we found an overturned Bradley with some shaken soldiers, and went right to work ensuring that the soldiers were okay, praying with them, and informing the commander that there were no serious casualties.

The bottom line: No matter what the obstacle or obstruction, press on unless otherwise directed by the Lord. Those can be placed in our way to test us to see if we really mean business.

## Obstacle or Obstruction?

Obstacles and obstructions can be turned into opportunities. Occasions like the BFV mission I just described allow us to grow and trust in God. He can even use roadblocks to steer us in another direction that normally we would not take.

Often God allows hard obstacles to be placed in our way so we might be trained to look to Him in all things. God wants us to be strong in the face of adversity.

Military special operations forces such as Navy Seals, Army Rangers, Green Berets and Marine Special Operations are trained to face the most demanding circumstances in combat. To that end their training is the most rigorous of all military forces. The failure rate is high. Leaders are looking for those who will not give up or give in. They purposely place obstacles and obstructions in the way to separate the best from the rest—because when the going gets really tough, the military call in special forces.

To complete Army Ranger School, a soldier must overcome seemingly insurmountable challenges under simulated battle conditions. The extreme physical intensity of this program, combined with the lack of sleep and the consumption of minimal calories, causes many students to lose twenty to thirty pounds or more. Completing this training is a true testament to a soldier's drive and determination. When this outstanding accomplishment is achieved, a graduate can proudly wear and display the well-deserved Ranger Tab.

I have not personally been through this type of training, but I have supported special operations forces (SOF) throughout my career in various capacities. And I have many close friends who have gone through the training. One of them told me that he prayed God would break his leg on an airborne jump so he would not have to complete Army Ranger School. It is that tough. Another friend found an old can of Spam filled with maggots on a beach in the swamp phase of Army Ranger School training. He calmly removed the maggots and consumed the contents. He was that hungry.

Today we do not prepare people for the spiritual warfare they are often fighting during the week. Many worshipers come to church on Sunday weary and sometimes discouraged. They hear the Word of God, fellowship with each other, get energized and leave church feeling great. But during the week they face the obstacles and obstructions alone in their daily lives. The lack of spiritual training is a sure recipe for defeat and disaster as end-times events begin unfolding at a quickening rate.

Christians in the West tend to think everything is going to continue hunky-dory and wonderful; when adversity hits, we are not ready for it. This will be especially true as we face the most difficult days in the history of mankind. This is why we need to view the obstacles and obstructions we face in life as opportunities for spiritual growth and training.

Jesus stated that "we know that we are children of God, and that the whole world is under the control of the evil one" (1 John 5:19). And we forget that "we aren't fighting against human enemies but against rulers, authorities, forces of cosmic darkness, and spiritual powers of evil in the heavens" (Ephesians 6:12 CEB).

Is there a difference between obstacles and obstructions?

An obstacle is something that blocks one's way or prevents or hinders progress. It is something in the way that can be avoided—for example, a pile of bricks in the middle of a road. Some synonyms for the word *obstacle* include *barrier, hurdle, stumbling block, hindrance, complication, difficulty, problem* and *disadvantage*. Do these terms mean something to you? Have you experienced them?

The definition of *obstruction* is slightly different. An obstruction is something blocking a passage—usually completely. An obstruction needs to be removed or expelled for the passage to be unblocked.

I have discovered that obstacles can be blessings in disguise. But many times I have gone down a path only to find an obstruction in the way. During those times I look to God for answers. It may be that He does not want me to go any farther down that road. It may be that I need to wait until the way is cleared.

Either way, obstacle or obstruction, it is important for us to develop such a relationship with God that we hear Him speaking to us about what to do next.

According to a Department of Defense publication, there are many principles you can employ to mitigate obstacles and obstructions that are in your way. The primary phrase found throughout this document is *assured mobility*.[5] This means being able to prepare, detect, manage, predict and maneuver around or through obstacles. At the end of this chapter are military and Christian "assured mobility" principles.

Now let's explore the life of one of the greatest spiritual warriors in the Bible and how he dealt with opposition, obstacles and obstructions.

## The Mighty Warrior Elijah

The prophet Elijah knew all about "assured mobility," even though he did not call it that in his day. Here is a mighty man of God who brought down kings and queens, stopped rain from falling on Israel for more than three years, and performed some of the greatest miracles in the Bible. Many scholars suspect he will come back in the end times as one of the two witnesses from the book of Revelation.

Revelation 11:3–6 (CEB) talks about these enigmatic figures:

"I will allow my two witnesses to prophesy for one thousand two hundred sixty days, wearing mourning clothes.

These are the two olive trees and the two lampstands that stand before the Lord of the earth. If anyone wants to hurt them, fire comes out of their mouth and burns up their enemies. So if anyone wants to hurt them, they have to be killed in this way. They have the power to close up the sky so that no rain will fall for as long as they prophesy. They also have power over the waters, to turn them into blood, and to strike the earth with any plague, as often as they wish."

Notice that the two witnesses perform miracles like those that Elijah performed on earth. Through God's power, the prophet not only stopped the rain, but brought down fire from heaven that killed more than one hundred soldiers (see 2 Kings 1:1–15). Also note that Elijah never died; he was taken up to heaven alive on a chariot of fire drawn by fiery horses (see 2 Kings 2:11–12).

Elijah faced some of the greatest opposition, obstacles and obstructions in the history of Israel. Israel, as a nation, had turned from God to worship the idols Baal and Asherah. Jezebel, the queen of Israel and wife of the notoriously evil king Ahab, routinely killed the prophets of God. Both Ahab and Jezebel wanted Elijah dead, but God supernaturally protected him for more than three years.

Then one of the greatest showdowns in Israel's history occurred. Many in Israel, plus 450 prophets of Baal, showed up on Mount Carmel to see what Elijah would do in the face of opposition. Elijah challenged the prophets to a showdown as to whose God would send down fire from heaven on the sacrifices they had prepared. "How long will you not decide between two choices?" he demanded. "If the LORD is the true God, follow him, but if Baal is the true God, follow him!" (1 Kings 18:21 NCV).

What happened next was unbelievable. The prophets of Baal prayed all day long, shouted and cut themselves, and nothing happened. No fire came from heaven to burn up their sacrifice.

Then Elijah prepared his sacrifice. To make the contest even harder, he soaked the sacrifice and wood with four jars of water three times, "so the water ran off the altar and filled the ditch" (verse 35). Then he approached the altar.

> "LORD, you are the God of Abraham, Isaac, and Israel," he prayed. "Prove that you are the God of Israel and that I am your servant. Show these people that you commanded me to do all these things. LORD, answer my prayer so these people will know that you, LORD, are God and that you will change their minds." Then fire from the LORD came down and burned the sacrifice, the wood, the stones, and the ground around the altar. It also dried up the water in the ditch. When all the people saw this, they fell down to the ground, crying, "The LORD is God! The LORD is God!"
>
> Verses 36–39

Elijah was not afraid of the obstacles and obstructions in his path—a wicked king and queen and the power of Baal worship in Israel—but took advantage of that opportunity to show off the power of God.

In these end times we need to go to the next level and take advantage of the obstacles in our way to show the world that God really exists and that He can overcome all things with the power of His Word.

## End-Times Challenges

Here are some of the end-times obstacles and obstructions we will face:

- Continued movement away from Christian values and norms.
- Social upheaval in the form of anti-Christian bias and persecution.
- Political unrest and movements to the extreme left.
- Government regulations that will target churches and synagogues.
- Families split over religion and politics.
- Advances in technology that will disrupt our daily lives.
- Continued moves away from biblical sexuality.

The New Testament writers foresaw these developments thousands of years ago:

- *Deception.* The Spirit clearly says that in latter times some people will turn away from the faith. They will pay attention to spirits that deceive and to the teaching of demons (1 Timothy 4:1 CEB).
- *Godlessness.* Understand that the last days will be dangerous times. People will be selfish and love money. They will be the kind of people who brag and who are proud. They will slander others, and they will be disobedient to their parents. They will be ungrateful, unholy, unloving, contrary, and critical. They will be without self-control and brutal, and they won't love what is good. They will be people who are disloyal, reckless, and conceited. They will love pleasure instead of loving God. They will look like they are religious but deny God's power. Avoid people like this (2 Timothy 3:1–5 CEB).
- *Mockery.* Most important, know this: in the last days scoffers will come, jeering, living by their own cravings, and saying, "Where is the promise of his coming?

After all, nothing has changed—not since the beginning of creation, nor even since the ancestors died" (2 Peter 3:3–4 CEB).

## MILITARY MOBILITY PRINCIPLES

Some military imperatives for "assured mobility" are:

* *Predict*. Engineers and planners predict potential enemy impediments to mobility by analyzing the enemy's tactics, techniques, procedures, capability and evolution.

* *Detect*. Engineers and planners use intelligence, surveillance and reconnaissance assets to identify the location of natural and manmade obstacles; to create and put into place obstacles against the enemy; and identify potential means for obstacle creation.

* *Prevent*. Engineers and other planners limit the enemy's ability to limit mobility through proactive measures before the obstacles are placed or activated.

* *Avoid*. If prevention fails, the commander will maneuver forces to avoid impediments to mobility.

* *Respond*. Response must be flexible and adaptable to operational capabilities, including a well-developed public information operations component.

## BELIEVER'S MOBILITY PRINCIPLES

* *Predict*. Analyze the enemy's tactics, techniques, procedures, capability and evolution. Know where the enemy might strike in your life. Take preventive measures.

★ *Detect.* Identify the location of supernatural and manmade obstacles. This includes in the church where you are most vulnerable to obstacles from the people you most love—a favorite enemy tactic. Be alert to personal weaknesses and avoid being set up.

★ *Prevent.* Limit the enemy's ability to influence you or your family through proactive measures before obstacles are put into place or activated. One example: anticipating upcoming big changes in life like marriage, retirement, a new job or graduation. Change is inevitable. What is important is what you do with it.

★ *Avoid.* Try to avoid impediments to mobility by anticipating potential obstacles or obstructions. An example of avoidance is when the disciples lowered the apostle Paul over the city wall at night to avoid his possible death at the hands of religious zealots (see Acts 9:25). Sometimes obstacles are not avoidable, and the Lord will see you through.

★ *Respond.* Your response to obstacles must be in the power and strength of the Lord. Get a holy anointing by prayer and plow through!

## STRATEGIC SPIRITUAL EXERCISES

Here are some practical takeaways to overcoming obstacles in your life:

1. What obstacles or obstructions have occurred in your life and how are those experiences helping you now?

2. Study the life of Elijah and find ways to emulate him.

3. Read biographies of spiritual heroes who have over-come obstacles in their lives.

4. Do some physical and spiritual preparedness work to get ready for the end times.

# PART 3

# ADVANCED TACTICS

# 13

# WEAPONS AND FIREPOWER

The weapons of our warfare are not carnal, but mighty in God for pulling down strongholds.

—2 Corinthians 10:4 NKJV

*NIGHT, Combined Arms Live Fire Range, Grafenwoehr Training Area, Grafenwöhr, Germany, early 1990s.* It is cold as I sit in one of the open hatches of an M1A1 Abrams tank—72 tons of steel with a devastating 120mm smooth-bore cannon, bristling with machine guns and a 1,500–horse-power turbine engine. This thing is a beast.

I am witnessing for the first time how much firepower a tank company can bring to a fight. Wow. As the tanks let go with the tremendous roar of 120mm rounds, two Apache helicopters hover close-by, one on my right and the other on my left, lighting up the sky with folding-fin 2.75–inch aerial rockets.

The combined firepower I am witnessing up close and personal will never leave me. I would not want to be on the receiving end of this barrage.

The U.S. Army has boatloads of weapons, armor, ammunition and ordnance. All those weapons will not win a war, however, without those who operate the equipment. Because the basic weapon in the Army is the soldier. And the soldier's primary offensive weapon is the rifle, currently the M4 carbine.

Almost every infantry soldier carries one or more weapons into battle. And with that weapon comes the basic load of ammunition—about three hundred rounds. Without his or her primary weapon and basic load, a soldier cannot perform the critical tasks of tactical offense. No warrior ever won a battle without a weapon, even if that weapon is himself or herself.

## End-Times Weapons

One of the signs that we are in the end times is the proliferation of weapons of mass destruction. There are so many new and devastating weapons that we can hardly touch on the subject in this chapter.

The book of Revelation, along with Ezekiel 38–39, tells us that literally billions of people will die before the return of the Lord. Along with many Bible scholars, I believe the following verses depict scenes from the battle of Armageddon:

"In my zeal and fiery wrath I declare that at that time there shall be a great earthquake in the land of Israel. The fish in the sea, the birds in the sky, the beasts of the field, every creature that moves along the ground, and all the people on the face of the earth will tremble at my presence. The mountains will be overturned, the cliffs will crumble and every wall will fall to the ground. I will summon a sword against Gog on all my mountains, declares the Sovereign LORD. Every man's sword will be against his brother. I will execute judgment on him with plague and bloodshed; I will pour down torrents of rain, hailstones and burning sulfur on him and on his troops and on the many nations with him. And so I will show my greatness and my holiness, and I will make myself known in the sight of many nations. Then they will know that I am the LORD."

Ezekiel 38:19–23

Look at Revelation 8:7–13 for a parallel version of this event:

The first angel sounded his trumpet, and there came hail and fire mixed with blood, and it was hurled down on the earth. A third of the earth was burned up, a third of the trees were burned up, and all the green grass was burned up. The second angel sounded his trumpet, and something like a huge mountain, all ablaze, was thrown into the sea. A third of the sea turned into blood, a third of the living creatures in the sea died, and a third of the ships were destroyed. The third angel sounded his trumpet, and a great star, blazing like a torch, fell from the sky on a third of the rivers and on the springs of water—the name of the star is Wormwood. A third of the waters turned bitter, and many people died from the waters that had become bitter. The fourth angel sounded his trumpet, and a third of the sun was struck, a third of the moon, and a third of the stars, so that a third of them turned dark. A third of the day was without light, and also a third of the night. As I watched, I heard an eagle that was flying in midair call out in a loud voice: "Woe! Woe! Woe to the inhabitants of the earth, because of the trumpet blasts about to be sounded by the other three angels!"

These verses depict mass destruction on a global scale never seen before, and this is just the beginning of the judgments of God on the earth during the Great Tribulation and before the return of Jesus Christ.

Some weapons that have already been used on our planet, as well as unimaginably destructive ones that have not yet been used, are implicated in the above verses. Such weapons include chemical weapons, biological warfare weapons, hydrogen bombs, fission (atomic) bombs, neutron bombs, toxicological weapons, radiological weapons, pure fusion bombs, boosted fission weapons and many others. Add the artificial intelligence weapons coming online, such as mass drone swarms, and you have a horrifying glimpse of what is coming to planet earth.

"As a practical matter, there are nations in the world that have the ability to decimate," says my friend retired U.S. Army Lieutenant General Ken Dahl. "They have the ability to end the existence of millions of people in America's cities and other countries. Russia could do that. China could do that. Both have a vast number of 'proven capability' [weapons of mass destruction] that we would not be able to defend ourselves against."[1]

## Weapons of Our Warfare

Despite the threat, many Christians today are powerless and weaponless. It seems there is a dearth of powerful warriors of God.

You can attend Christian concerts, seminars, workshops and worship services with the latest worship music, and it will not transform you into the kind of warrior God intends you to be. Second Corinthians 10:4 (NKJV) says: "The weapons of our warfare are not carnal but mighty in God for pulling down strongholds." Notice that it says *weapons*, meaning there is more than one.

Often when we think of spiritual weapons, we recall that God's Word, the Bible, is our sword, but Scripture tells of many weapons—spiritual weapons that are mighty through God's strength, not our own. As we learn to tap into the power of the Holy Spirit and use these weapons, we will see examples of supernatural victory in our lives.

Evangelist John Ramirez, a former satanic high priest, says:

> God taught me that the weapons of His warfare are indestructible in the spirit realm, and how to use them—how to fight in the devil's camp, how to uproot, how to cast down, how to break the patterns and cycles of the enemy Take my word for it. The devil's got nothing on you. You can get back what he has stolen from you and then some, but it's time to confront. It's time to be the Church.[2]

## The Full Armor

Back in chapter 6, we identified seven pieces of armor:

> Stand therefore, having your waist girded with truth, having put on the breastplate of righteousness, having your feet fitted with the readiness of the gospel of peace, and above all, taking the shield of faith, with which you will be able to extinguish all the fiery arrows of the evil one. Take the helmet of salvation and the sword of the Spirit, which is the word of God. Pray in the Spirit always with all kinds of prayer and supplication. To that end be alert with all perseverance and supplication for all the saints.
>
> Ephesians 6:14–18 MEV

Here are the spiritual weapons in this passage:

- The belt of truth
- The breastplate of righteousness

- The shoes of the Gospel of peace
- The shield of faith
- The helmet of salvation
- The sword of the Spirit
- Praying in the Spirit

## Worship

In chapter 9 we discussed another weapon at our disposal. When Jehoshaphat, king of Judah, faced a vast enemy army, he sent worshipers ahead of his own army, who sang and praised God—and the enemy was defeated without a fight. Read the astonishing story in 2 Chronicles 20. True worship, a condition of heart that elevates God above everything else, is a powerful weapon to fight the enemy.

## The Name of Jesus

Here is the weapon of the name of Jesus:

> God exalted him to the highest place and gave him the name that is above every name, that at the name of Jesus every knee should bow, in heaven and on earth and under the earth, and every tongue acknowledge that Jesus Christ is Lord, to the glory of God the Father.
>
> Philippians 2:9–11

The name of Jesus has incredible power. Demons are defenseless before the name of Jesus (see Luke 10:17). Healing occurs in Jesus' name (see Acts 3:6–8, 16; 4:10). Everything we do and say should be done in Jesus' name (see Colossians 3:17). Jesus invited and commanded us to pray in His name, and He promised incredible results: "You may ask me for anything in my name, and I will do it" (John 14:13).

### Your Own Testimony

Your testimony is another highly effective spiritual weapon. Christians during the Tribulation will overcome the forces of darkness "by the blood of the Lamb and by the word of their testimony" (Revelation 12:11). When the enemy gets you focused on negative things, remember your testimony—all the miracles God has performed in your life and all the times He has provided for and helped you when it seemed as if you would not make it.

### Prayer

An Old Testament story illustrates another powerful weapon of warfare. Joshua, the leader of the Israelite army, was facing the joint forces of five Canaanite kings, when the Lord threw the enemy armies into confusion and they fled from Israel. Even then Joshua was not afraid to employ the weapon of prayer in the battlefield:

> Joshua said to the LORD in the presence of Israel: "Sun, stand still over Gibeon, and you, moon, over the Valley of Aijalon." So the sun stood still, and the moon stopped, till the nation avenged itself on its enemies, as it is written in the Book of Jashar. The sun stopped in the middle of the sky and delayed going down about a full day. There has never been a day like it before or since, a day when the LORD listened to a human being. Surely the LORD was fighting for Israel!
>
> Joshua 10:12–14

If you aspire to be an effective end-times weapon of God, make it a practice to pray constantly, because prayer is one of our most powerful spiritual weapons. Often people will turn to everything else *except* prayer, thinking they don't want to "bother" God. So we use prayer as a last resort, a 911 emergency call for help, instead of the first thing we do. This is a form of satanic deception. It is impossible to bother God! That is a lie of Satan, because God is omnipotent and omniscient—infinite in power and possessing unlimited knowledge. Our primary weapon should be speaking to God about everything we do, all the time, not just as a nuclear option in a crisis.

Prayer should not be the last button we push, but the first, and we must use it all the time. The apostle Paul told us to "pray without ceasing" (1 Thessalonians 5:17). Spiritual warriors know how to acquire and use this power to assault the forces of evil. Prayer is a powerful weapon that should be the first weapon in our inventory, and one we practice constantly. We should always be online with God in prayer.

## Spiritual Firepower

On my first Blackhawk helicopter mission out of Fort Ord, California, I was in the back of the bird on a headset with the pilots in the cockpit. They decided to fly to Monterey Bay, where we saw anchored below us the USS Missouri, one of the Navy's last and largest battleships. It was there to celebrate the Navy's Fleet Week.

I was mesmerized by the size and weaponry of this ship. Suddenly I noticed that some of its gun turrets were tracking us. Those gun turrets were MK 15 Phalanx CIWS, a close-in weapon system for defense against airborne threats such as anti-ship missiles and helicopters (yes, Blackhawks included). That system can spew out a wall of steel from a radar-guided 20-millimeter Vulcan cannon mounted on a swiveling base at a rate of 4,500 rounds a minute.[3]

I was shocked and spoke quickly to the pilots. "Guys, I think those guns are locked on and following us."

They had noticed, too, and we were out of there in seconds.

A while later we found out by talking to the ship's captain that, although the radar was indeed tracking us, no rounds had been loaded into that system while in port. Thank the Lord!

The point is, that ship was always on and ready for war, even at home port. It was tracking all movements around it—on the sea and in the air.

We should be, too!

I have said repeatedly that soldiers need to train as if they are fighting in real combat. The military goes to great lengths to put them into realistic combat scenarios to set the conditions for success in war. It is of no use to possess lethal firepower if you don't use it.

What does this have to do with you? Everything! In the end times, it does not matter how often you study the Bible, read your daily devotional or even go to church, if you are not putting into practice what you are learning. "Put into practice what you learned from me," wrote the apostle Paul, "what you heard and saw and realized. Do that, and God, who makes everything work together, will work you into his most excellent harmonies" (Philippians 4:9 MSG).

The first-century Church carried spiritual firepower with them and used it all the time. We must do the same, and even more so during these increasingly perilous times.

As Pastor John Wimber, founder of Vineyard USA, famously asked, "When do we get to do all the stuff?" Wimber had been saved recently and asked a lay leader at a church, "When do we get to do the stuff? You know, the stuff here in the Bible, the stuff Jesus did, like healing the sick, raising the dead, healing the blind—stuff like that."

He was told that they did not do that anymore.

John replied, "You mean I gave up drugs for that?"[4]

As end-times events accelerate, we need to do what Jesus did *and* what Joshua did. Joshua asked the Lord to stop the sun and moon, acted on what God told him to do, and then saw the supernatural unfold before his eyes.

Later the first-century Church practiced the power of God working through them in miraculous ways to change the world. We need to be doing the same things today that our brothers and sisters did thousands of years ago.

## MILITARY FIREPOWER PRINCIPLES

- ⋆ *Firepower* provides the destructive force essential to overcoming the enemy's ability and will to fight. Firepower and military maneuvers complement each other.

- ⋆ *Maneuvers* employ forces to achieve a position of advantage over the enemy to accomplish the mission.

- ⋆ *Leadership.* Because it deals directly with soldiers, leadership is the most dynamic element of combat power.

- ⋆ *Force protection* minimizes the effects of enemy firepower and intelligence. Protection is neither timidity nor risk avoidance.

- ⋆ *Information.* The common operational picture (COP) is based on the best information and reconnaissance, giving commanders an accurate, near real-time perspective and knowledge of the battlefield situation.

## BELIEVER'S FIREPOWER PRINCIPLES

- ⋆ *Firepower* is provided by the Holy Spirit, the destructive force essential to overcoming the enemy's ability and will to fight. "My message and my preaching were not in persuasive words of wisdom, but in demonstration of the Spirit and of power" (1 Corinthians 2:4 NASB).

* *Maneuvers* are following hard after God, listening to His directions so we can achieve a position of advantage over the enemy to accomplish the mission.
* *Leadership.* Because it deals directly with believers, leadership is the most dynamic element of combat power. Jesus is the leader; you are the soldier.
* *Force protection* minimizes the effects of enemy firepower, maneuvers and information from our enemies.
* *Information.* God has you and the common operational picture (COP) in His hand. Walk by faith.

## STRATEGIC SPIRITUAL EXERCISES

Here are some practical takeaways to help you use God's firepower in your life:

1. Next time you encounter a tough situation, go to the Lord first and use His unlimited power.
2. Learn the weapons in your inventory—how they work; how to use them; and how other people have used and are using them.
3. Continue to ask God for His protection in all things.
4. Rely on God and inquire of Him about information you may not know. "Call to Me, and I will answer you, and show you great and mighty things, which you do not know" (Jeremiah 33:3 NKJV).

# 14

# PREPPING FOR THE END TIMES

"Suppose a king is about to go to war against another king. Won't he first sit down and consider whether he is able with ten thousand men to oppose the one coming against him with twenty thousand?"

—Luke 14:31

WINTER 2006, *near the Hindu Kush mountain range in Afghanistan.* We are headed through vast minefields on either side of the road to some of the Pashtun tribes who are badly in need of warm winter clothing and shoes. Our convoy is heavily guarded with front and aft gun trucks as we approach tribal territory. We are loaded with as many goods as we can carry. I notice children running around the mountainous area with no shoes on this bitter cold day, and my heart breaks.

We have interpreters and liaison personnel with us who have done this sort of mission many times before. This is my first one. We have been told during the pre-mission planning session to allow the liaisons to talk to the tribal chiefs first so there will be no trouble with crowds stampeding us, causing injuries or even our deaths. I take great joy knowing that our team is handing out scores of coats, blankets, shoes, pants and other items. Most of these have been donated by churches back home.

My battalion chaplain—then Captain—Scott Koeman, spent months planning this. The plan is not only to help the tribes, but to continue friendly relations with the tribal chiefs and warlords.

As I stand back and watch the scenario unfold, I cannot help but remember that we need each other's help on this planet. It also occurs to me that if it were not for the grace of God, we, too, could be in the same situation in the future as the end times progress toward Armageddon—a tribe of people in the midst of a bloody war in need of food and clothes with no money to buy anything and no place to run.

## Physical Preparation

Logistics, in the words of Prussian general Carl von Clausewitz, is getting the force to the "fight at the right place and the right time."[1] The military takes seriously the need for logistical support in combat. Many armies over the centuries have gone into combat without the right equipment and supplies—and perished.

The elite and storied 82nd Airborne Division must have enough supplies on hand to sustain airborne combat operations (meaning parachuting out of airplanes into combat) for about 36 hours. After that, if no logistical support is available, its fighting capability is cut drastically. They need the three Bs: beans, bullets and Band-Aids (food, ammo and medical supplies).

Let's put it bluntly: If you don't have enough food, water, bullets and basic necessities, you cannot win a war.

The Germans in World War II discovered this the hard way. Its army overextended itself in its march to Stalingrad, Russia. It outpaced its own supply lines and, in the end, could not sustain its massive force, even with the German Luftwaffe (air force) dropping supplies to them from the air. The Russians eventually surrounded the Sixth Army German forces with better equipped, better fed and better clothed soldiers in the Battle of Stalingrad during the winter of 1942–1943. On January 31, 1943, Germany surrendered. Casualties were massive.

### Emergency Preparedness

We have focused for most of this book on spiritual and mental preparation for the end of days. But we are human beings and have physical needs. We hunger, thirst and get tired. And you don't have to be a genius to see that viral pandemics and natural disasters are already wreaking havoc on planet earth. We hear about hurricanes, tsunamis, tornadoes, floods, fires, earthquakes, storms and volcanoes. It is only prudent to have the necessities on hand.

Having an emergency preparedness kit is a must. It should include the following items:[2]

- Water—one gallon of water per person per day for at least three days, for drinking and sanitation
- Non-perishable food—at least a three-day supply
- Toilet paper, disinfectant
- Battery-powered or hand-crank radio and a NOAA weather radio with tone alert
- Flashlight

- First-aid kit
- Extra batteries
- Whistle to signal for help
- Dust mask to help filter contaminated air
- Plastic sheeting and duct tape to shelter in place
- Moist towelettes, garbage bags and plastic ties for personal sanitation
- Wrench or pliers to turn off utilities
- Manual can opener for food
- Local maps
- Cellphone with chargers and a backup battery

This list covers only the basics for a short duration. A more complete list appears in the appendix, "Prioritized Checklist for the End Times," at the end of this book. When the Antichrist comes to power, the global economy starts to fail, nations go to war against other nations, and natural and manmade disasters strike, that is when serious prior planning will be vital to survival.

### Other Considerations

It is important to note that prepping goes well beyond our own individual or family needs. God put us here to be able to help others in need, too. Some people will undertake extensive preparations for the last days. There are many things to think about in terms of the next steps in this process.

It should be noted that some people in recent years have given prepping a bad name. The kind of prepping we are referring to does not involve some anarchist desire to overthrow the government, but the type of preparation necessary for survival in the last days, so we can share with and care for each other. In the military, going to war involves a logistical plan to stock up on the right amount of food, ammunition and equipment. That logistical and prudent plan is another term for prepping.

Depending on whether you live in an urban or rural area, we recommend water resources that include filtration systems, firearms for hunting and protection, a garden, solar power generation (including generators), underground shelters, long-term food storage, money management (yes, it is wise to pay off all your debts as soon as possible), and a host of other recommendations available in the appendix of this book. These are important things to know and think about as we race toward the future.

"Number one, you should be healthy," says Ken Dahl, former commanding general at IMCOM. He explains:

> Your physical health, your mental health and your spiritual health are paramount. You can't invest in those things when a disaster comes. It's a little late. Here comes a forest fire. Here comes a tsunami. Here comes whatever—a pandemic. It's too late. If you're going to endure hardship, it's going to stress your body and your mind, so you need to have a body and mind prepared and ready. And that is something—physical exercise, spiritual disciplines and mental conditioning—you need to do every single day. If you're not doing that, and you're vulnerable or weak, then you will likely succumb. It's just that simple. So that's what the daily investment is all about.[3]

Here are some scriptural admonitions about preparing:

- Luke 14:28: "Suppose one of you wants to build a tower. Won't you first sit down and estimate the cost to see if you have enough money to complete it?"

- Proverbs 15:22: Plans fail for lack of counsel, but with many advisers they succeed.
- Proverbs 21:5: The plans of the diligent lead to profit as surely as haste leads to poverty.
- Proverbs 6:6–8: Go to the ant, you sluggard; consider its ways and be wise! It has no commander, no overseer or ruler, yet it stores its provisions in summer and gathers its food at harvest.

In contrast to the last proverb—about the ant gathering food during the summer since winter is coming—some people say to themselves, *Well, when it comes to it, God will supply my needs and take care of me in the midst of trouble.* Our answer: What if God is using this book to tell you to prepare?

The first-century Church had to come together to distribute food:

> In those days when the number of disciples was increasing, the Hellenistic Jews among them complained against the Hebraic Jews because their widows were being overlooked in the daily distribution of food.
>
> Acts 6:1

We do not want to minimize what the Almighty can do. He certainly can and will intervene. But consider another proverb: "The prudent see danger and take refuge; but the simple keep going and pay the penalty" (Proverbs 22:3). And God will give us wisdom as He did for Joseph, who saved a nation by storing food during seven years of plenty prior to seven years of famine:

> The seven years of abundance in Egypt came to an end, and the seven years of famine began, just as Joseph had

said. There was famine in all the other lands, but in the whole land of Egypt there was food. When all Egypt began to feel the famine, the people cried to Pharaoh for food. Then Pharaoh told all the Egyptians, "Go to Joseph and do what he tells you." When the famine had spread over the whole country, Joseph opened all the storehouses and sold grain to the Egyptians, for the famine was severe throughout Egypt. And all the world came to Egypt to buy grain from Joseph, because the famine was severe everywhere.

Genesis 41:53–57

## Biblical Insights

God is aware of our physical limitations and frailties. Not all believers will survive the end times. Many will be martyred during the Great Tribulation:

> When he opened the fifth seal, I saw under the altar the souls of those who had been slain because of the word of God and the testimony they had maintained. They called out in a loud voice, "How long, Sovereign Lord, holy and true, until you judge the inhabitants of the earth and avenge our blood?"

Revelation 6:9–10

These martyrs are taken gloriously into heaven:

> After this I looked, and there before me was a great multitude that no one could count, from every nation, tribe, people and language, standing before the throne and before the Lamb. They were wearing white robes and were holding palm branches in their hands. . . . Then one of the elders asked me, "These in white robes—who are they, and where did they come from?" I answered, "Sir, you know." And he

said, "These are they who have come out of the great tribulation; they have washed their robes and made them white in the blood of the Lamb."

Revelation 7:9, 13–14

Even so, we must all be prepared to endure until we are either called home through death or the Rapture—the literal taking away of the believer from the earth in an instant.

I personally believe in a pre-wrath Rapture, meaning it will happen before the wrath of God is poured out upon the earth. I also believe, however, that first we will see the rise of the Antichrist and the great rebellion against God:

> Concerning the coming of our Lord Jesus Christ and our being gathered to him, we ask you, brothers and sisters, not to become easily unsettled or alarmed by the teaching allegedly from us—whether by a prophecy or by word of mouth or by letter—asserting that the day of the Lord has already come. Don't let anyone deceive you in any way, for that day will not come until the rebellion occurs and the man of lawlessness is revealed, the man doomed to destruction.
>
> 2 Thessalonians 2:1–3

When the Rapture happens is up for debate, but it will happen in the Lord's timing.

### Sharing

We must be prepared to help the Jewish people who will be persecuted along with the Church. Just as some Germans helped and supported the Jews during World War II, we need to be there to support them, now and at the end of the age.

Some do not understand the following passage:

"When the Son of Man comes in his glory, and all the angels with him, he will sit on his glorious throne. All the nations will be gathered before him, and he will separate the people one from another as a shepherd separates the sheep from the goats. He will put the sheep on his right and the goats on his left. Then the King will say to those on his right, 'Come, you who are blessed by my Father; take your inheritance, the kingdom prepared for you since the creation of the world. For I was hungry and you gave me something to eat, I was thirsty and you gave me something to drink, I was a stranger and you invited me in, I needed clothes and you clothed me, I was sick and you looked after me, I was in prison and you came to visit me.' Then the righteous will answer him, 'Lord, when did we see you hungry and feed you, or thirsty and give you something to drink? When did we see you a stranger and invite you in, or needing clothes and clothe you? When did we see you sick or in prison and go to visit you?' The King will reply, 'Truly I tell you, whatever you did for one of the least of these brothers and sisters of mine, you did for me.'"

Matthew 25:31–40

Many apply this passage to generally helping the poor and downtrodden, but one cannot be saved or go to heaven just because they were generous. We think it is clear that our Lord is speaking about helping Jewish people (the hungry, thirsty and those in prison) in the end times. The context of the passage is the judgment of all peoples living at that time. And in the context of "the least of these brothers and sisters of mine," I think the Lord is going to judge the nations on their treatment of Israel, the Jews, during the end times, and especially during the persecution by the Antichrist. There will be others as well who refuse the mark of the Beast and are either killed or persecuted.[4]

## Supernatural Provision

At the same time, there are many examples in Scripture of God supernaturally taking care of His people. Elijah, one of the great warriors in the Kingdom of God, was fed supernaturally after he faced a death threat from Queen Jezebel and ran for his life:

> He himself went a day's journey into the wilderness, and came and sat down under a broom tree. And he prayed that he might die, and said, "It is enough! Now, LORD, take my life, for I am no better than my fathers!" Then as he lay and slept under a broom tree, suddenly an angel touched him, and said to him, "Arise and eat." Then he looked, and there by his head was a cake baked on coals, and a jar of water. So he ate and drank, and lay down again. And the angel of the LORD came back the second time, and touched him, and said, "Arise and eat, because the journey is too great for you." So he arose, and ate and drank; and he went in the strength of that food forty days and forty nights as far as Horeb, the mountain of God.
>
> 1 Kings 19:4–8 NKJV

God gave Elijah the nutrition he needed in the middle of nowhere to sustain him for the next mission.

In the not-too-distant future, there may be times when we, too, will need that kind of divine provision to survive. So let's take precautions now to be smart about the coming days.

You may not live in a rural place, or out in the country where you can live off the land, raise livestock and grow vegetable gardens or fields of wheat. But wherever you live, there are ways you can prepare for the future and make contingency plans for natural and manmade disasters.

Joel Richardson, author and filmmaker, notes that if you do not store up food and other supplies and prepare for calamities, the Bible calls you a "fool" (see Proverbs 21:20 and 27:12):

> If you see a storm coming and you don't prepare, you're a fool. When you see calamity coming and you don't prepare, you're a fool. That said, I think the heart of the issue is much more important than rice and beans and bullets. I'm convinced that with every tragedy, trial, season of pain and difficulty we face, the Lord is giving us an opportunity to embrace the lesson of John 15:5. Jesus said, "I am the vine," and we are just the branches. And "apart from Me, you can do nothing."[5]

One of the best examples of how believers should act in the last days, says Richardson, is Rees Howells, intercessor, missionary and founder of The Bible College of Wales. During World War II he housed orphans, trusted God and saw provision come in on a regular basis. Richardson continues:

> He didn't just build a bunker for his own survival; rather he built a home for the homeless and was able to become a shelter amid a period of chaos. I believe that's what the Lord wants His people to be in the last days—not people who build bunkers out of fear and anxiety, trying to figure out ways to protect their food from hungry neighbors, but those who are thinking how they can be more like Rees Howells or Dietrich Bonhoeffer or Corrie ten Boom, whose family saved Jews during the Holocaust and became a "hiding place" in the midst of the dark hour. We need to be those kinds of people. So we can study some of those great men and women

of recent history, and learn how we can be lighthouses and cities of refuge in the days ahead.[6]

The following tips will help you prepare for any number of calamities.

## MILITARY PREPPING PRINCIPLES[7]

* *Integration* is combining all the elements of sustainment (tasks, functions, systems, processes and organizations) with operations to ensure unity of command and effort.

* *Anticipation* is foreseeing operational requirements and initiating actions without waiting for an operation order.

* *Identifying* required support starts the process of acquiring the sustainment that best supports the operation.

* *Responsiveness* is the ability to react to changing requirements in order to maintain support.

* *Simplicity* relates to the procedures that minimize the complexity of sustainment. Clear tasks and clearly defined command relationships contribute to simplicity.

* *Economy* is providing sustainment resources in an efficient manner to enable a commander to employ all assets to achieve the greatest effect possible.

* *Survivability* consists of the military capability to avoid or withstand hostile actions or environmental conditions while retaining the ability to fulfill its primary mission.

* *Continuity* is the uninterrupted provision of sustainment across all levels of war.

* *Improvisation* is the ability to adapt sustainment operations to unexpected situations or circumstances affecting a mission.

## BELIEVER'S PREPPING PRINCIPLES

* *Integration.* It is important for you to work closely with other believers in sharing common goals and prepping ideas, goods, services, food, water and other resources. No one is an island.
* *Anticipation* is key in preparing for the future. What will you need to sustain yourself, family, friends and others in a natural or manmade disaster?
* *Identifying* required support starts the process of acquiring what will be needed to best support survival.
* *Responsiveness* is the ability to react to changing requirements and respond to meet the needs to maintain support. Physical and emotional support is an ever-changing requirement.
* *Simplify, simplify, simplify.* As things go south, what is really needed is the most important. It makes simplifying easy.
* *Economy* ensures that you have a sustainable operation—for example, rationing food and water to last the longest time.
* *Survivability* consists of quality of life over a long period. Plan on quality as well as quantity.
* *Continuity* is being able to live through to the Rapture and coming of the Lord.
* *Improvisation*, creativeness and invention. Be flexible, adaptable and adjustable to the changing environment.

## STRATEGIC SPIRITUAL EXERCISES

Here are some practical takeaways in preparing for the end times:

1. Start small and add to your provisions. Don't buy things you will not eat or drink over the long haul.
2. Your stockpile will need to be rotated and used. Nothing lasts forever.
3. Ask other preppers about their plans.
4. Remember, God is and will always be your source, even in the most difficult of times.
5. Plan on sharing with others.

# 15
# COMING HOME

Then they gathered the kings together to the place that in Hebrew is called Armageddon.

—Revelation 16:16

*SPRING 1992, 747 charter jet, circling over Biggs Army Airfield, El Paso, Texas.* I am reflecting on six-plus months of combat duty with the 43rd Air Defense Artillery Regiment in Saudi Arabia.

Coming home from months in a combat zone is always bittersweet. Bitter, because you are leaving part of yourself in the desert, and sweet, coming home to family and friends.

I am looking down over the airfield; there is a welcome home ceremony with a U.S. Army band, general officers, a crowd of well-wishers and families. I tear up. This is my second deployment in two years, the first being in the jungles of Honduras as the Joint Task Force–Bravo chaplain. I am war-weary and in need of rest and recuperation. I have put in literally thousands of road and air miles around Saudi Arabia, visiting, counseling, training and supporting our troops.

Let me tell you, there is nothing like coming home, although it takes time to readjust and reunite with family and friends and get used to a different routine.

I think it will be that way as we approach our time to be reunited with the Lord. We must not think of the place we are currently in as home; it is only temporary. Our future home is in heaven with the Father, Son and Holy Spirit, as well as with the vast company of saints and angels who populate that glorious place. And eventually, after the Millennium and the Great White Throne Judgment (see Revelation 20:11–15), our home will be in the New Jerusalem on a restored planet earth.

We must never forget that life on earth is short at best; and given biblical prophecies, we must keep an eternal perspective. God is waiting to reward us for our faithful service during our time on earth.

The apostle Paul said it best when he was nearing the end of his journey. Paul knew he was to be executed soon in Rome. He probably wrote his second letter to Timothy during a second imprisonment in Rome following a fourth missionary journey not recorded in Acts. Expecting that death would come soon, Paul wrote this farewell letter to his son in the faith, who was at Ephesus, urging him to stand firm. Here are his immortal and inspirational words:

> I have fought the good fight, I have finished the race, I have kept the faith. Now there is in store for me the crown of righteousness, which the Lord, the righteous Judge, will award to me on that day—and not only to me, but also to all who have longed for his appearing.
>
> 2 Timothy 4:7–8

Notice that he refers to the Second Coming of our Lord Jesus Christ. We must recognize that the end times are ultimately about phasing out the dominion of the god of this world and ushering in our Lord Jesus as the King of kings and Lord of lords.

## The Greatest Opportunity

In a recent Christmas sermon, Saddleback Church pastor Rick Warren—who was kind enough to offer to place a copy of *The Military Guide to Armageddon* in his Guinness World Records collection of books signed by the authors—told his congregation that in the newspaper business, the largest headline you can possibly use is called "Second Coming type font," for the obvious reason that it would be used after the Second Coming of Christ.

"The most cataclysmic, or the most important, or the most profound experience in history," he said, "will be the end of history when Jesus Christ comes back."[1]

Warren, author of the bestselling book *The Purpose Driven Life*—which sold fifty million copies, prompting *Time* magazine in 2005 to name him one of "the 100 most influential people in the world"—said that the Bible has

> far, far more [verses] about the Second Coming than the first coming. The Second Coming of Jesus is called the "blessed hope" . . . because when you really understand it, it gives you comfort, it gives you strength, it gives you confidence to face the future, it gives you hope. And then you know that no matter what's going to happen, you've read the final chapter of the Book. And I have read the final chapter of the Book. We win. Okay. We win. And He's coming back one day.
>
> Now, the night before Jesus was crucified, before He went to the cross, He said this to His disciples, in John 14:2–3: "I'm going to heaven to prepare a place for you, and after I

prepare a place for you, I will come back . . . to get you so that where I am, you will also be with Me." That's the greatest promise in Scripture. "If I go . . . I'm coming back." Did He go? Yeah, He went after the resurrection. Is He coming back? Absolutely.[2]

Christ's return is literally going to be the greatest event in history—the culmination of the grand biblical narrative that began in Genesis and concludes in Revelation. Believers must prepare for this pivotal event with eternity in mind. Why should people be ready? Because God wants His people to be involved in not just what He is doing on the earth, but in what He plans to do on the earth.

Rabbi Jonathan Bernis, president and CEO of Jewish Voice Ministries International and host of the globally syndicated television show "Jewish Voice with Jonathan Bernis," says:

> I think of the statement that the men of Issachar were wise because they "understood the times" (1 Chronicles 12:32). I love that verse. So I go beyond just that God wants us to prepare so we can escape whatever is ahead. He wants us to be involved. He wants you to be active. He wants you to be relevant voices. He wants you to be the ones who provide answers to people. He doesn't want us to be unaware of His return. We don't know the day, we don't know the hour, but we're implored to know the season.[3]

This is what Jesus told his disciples in Matthew 24:42–44:

> "Therefore keep watch, because you do not know on what day your Lord will come. But understand this: If the owner of the house had known at what time of night the thief was coming, he would have kept watch and would not have let

his house be broken into. So you also must be ready, because the Son of Man will come at an hour when you do not expect him."

As the world watches end-of-the-age biblical prophecies unfold, believers should spend even more time sharing their faith with others and in prayer and intercession for a lost world. Bernis continues:

> This is not about hiding away in a cave, waiting for Him to return. It's about being proactive, involved, co-working, active. We have a purpose. This is the greatest opportunity in history for followers of Jesus to be involved in God's eternal plan. There has never been a greater time to be alive, but we have to have "ears to hear and eyes to see" (Matthew 13:15).
>
> I think we should be actively carrying out whatever destiny God has given us, whatever role He's called us to play—in the marketplace, in funding ministries, in direct mission work, in evangelistic work or in aid work. And, of course, we need to be sharing our faith personally with the people around us—family, co-workers, neighbors. We have the only eternal answer and God cares about what happens to people for eternity.[4]

## A New Heaven and a New Earth

We saw in chapter 4 that the forces of darkness want to merge the nations into a one-world government in preparation for the Antichrist's rule. The plan is to end all wars and bring mankind into global unity. Almost every book I read at the U.S. Army War College spoke to the issue of a global government.

James Garrison, founder and president of State of the World Forum, says, "We are going to end up with world government. It's inevitable. . . .There's going to be conflict, coercion and consensus. That's all part of what will be required as we give birth to the first global civilization."[5]

It makes sense, after all, that if there were a one-world government, then the logical conclusion, according to globalists, is that there would be no more war. However, the opposite is true. Just as with socialism, Communism and dictatorships, the goal has always been to subject the masses to enslavement; and enslavement always leads to rebellion and war.

The truth is, no manmade government will work because of mankind's innate selfishness and sin. Even democracy cannot work without morality, and morality does not work without Christ. As there are forces at work trying to bring the nations together, we must be hard at work in preparing for that eventuality.

God foresaw all this in advance. In fact, the first prophecy in the Bible, Genesis 3:15, predicted what is unfolding now, as God spoke to Lucifer:

> "I will put enmity between you and the woman [Eve], and between your offspring and hers; he [Christ] will crush your head, and you will strike his heel."

Bernis points out about this passage:

> This is not a prophecy of the first coming of Christ; it's a prophecy of the first coming *and* the Second Coming. God's eternal plan for the redemption of mankind involves the full scope of redemption. The full scope of redemption involves the first coming and the return, so the Second Coming is critical to God fulfilling His plan for mankind to restore us to the time before the Fall of Adam. So it is essential, if we care about God's plan being fulfilled, that we care about the return [of Christ]. The Bible refers to this in Acts 3:21 as the

restoration of all things. If we want to see all things restored, then the Messiah has to come back.[6]

We have mentioned that, as we were finishing this book, the world was hit with a pandemic named coronavirus disease 2019, or COVID-19. It was unprecedented in terms of stopping the world in its tracks. The virus sickened more than six million people in a matter of months.[7] It upended the economic stability of the world, causing the stock market to fluctuate wildly. In some places, the military, because of its expertise and leadership, stepped in to supplement civilian medical personnel and facilities.

The hope, as we write, is that we will go back to normalcy soon. But the truth is, we are going to be living out a new normal from now on in ways we cannot imagine. For many the future is uncertain. But for the believer, the best is yet to come.

The end times are not about the end of mankind; they are the beginning of a glorious new future without the Fall of man, without the mark of sin, without the deceit of Satan, and without death, disease and destruction.

This guide is all about getting ready for the journey. It is a resounding alarm to prepare for coming world events and the inevitable conflicts that will arise in the last days before the return of Christ. And it is about becoming an end-times warrior of God as we witness the rise of evil never before experienced on this planet.

In Revelation 21:1–7 (NKJV) the apostle John paints a vivid description of the reward awaiting those who eagerly await His return:

Now I saw a new heaven and a new earth, for the first heaven and the first earth had passed away. Also there was no more sea. Then I, John, saw the holy city, New Jerusalem, coming down out of heaven from God, prepared as a bride adorned for her husband. And I heard a loud voice from heaven saying, "Behold, the tabernacle of God is with men, and He will dwell with them, and they shall be His people. God Himself will be with them and be their God. And God will wipe away every tear from their eyes; there shall be no more death, nor sorrow, nor crying. There shall be no more pain, for the former things have passed away."

Then He who sat on the throne said, "Behold, I make all things new." And He said to me, "Write, for these words are true and faithful."

And He said to me, "It is done! I am the Alpha and the Omega, the Beginning and the End. I will give of the fountain of the water of life freely to him who thirsts. He who overcomes shall inherit all things, and I will be his God and he shall be My son."

We are ready for the battle ahead and to go home to a new heaven and new earth. How about you?

# APPENDIX
## PRIORITIZED CHECKLIST FOR THE END TIMES

The following "prioritized checklist"—featuring military and Federal Emergency Management Agency (FEMA) disaster preparation guidelines—is a prepper's guide to help you get ready for the last days.

### PRE-DISASTER/PRE-TRIBULATION

* Water
  * *Supplies*
    * » FEMA recommends having access to one gallon of water per person per day for a minimum period of three days. That is three gallons of water per person.
    * » We recommend more than FEMA because you do not know how long it will be until you can get fresh water. Go with a minimum two gallons of water per day for five days, or ten gallons of water for each person.

» Purchase a quantity of commercial bottled water and drink by its use date. Keep rotating.

» High-grade rainwater barrels from a trusted filtrated source can be very handy in an emergency. Do your homework here; some have been known to leak.

» For longer periods, you will need the blue emergency, BPA-free, food-grade barrels in sizes from 15 gallons to as large as 320 gallons. The size needed would depend on the number of people and the length of time projected.

» For those who can afford it and have the outdoor space, there are also underground water cisterns that are quite large and can store water for long periods of time.

- *Filtration*

» There are many personal water filtration systems out there for a very reasonable price. These filters can purify 99.9 percent of all contaminants so you can safely drink water from puddles, ponds, lakes and almost all outdoor water sources.

» Home filtration systems. The best systems for the home are multi-stage reverse osmosis drinking water filter systems. If you still have running water at home and it has been contaminated, this system is a lifesaver. If you install one in your home, you will use it all year long and it will save you money on purchases of bottled water.

» Water purification tablets. You will have to wait for the tablet to work, anywhere from thirty minutes to four hours or more. There are tablets on the market that do not leave a foul taste. There are three main types of tablets: iodine (tetraglycine hydroperiodide), chlorine (sodium dichloroisocyanurate) and chlorine dioxide. Again, do your research online for the best and most effective tablets.

- *Sources (Will Need Filtration)*

» Groundwater (will need digging equipment).

» Rainwater.

» Canals.

» Wells.

» Puddles.

» Creeks.

» Streams.

» Ponds.

» Lakes.

» Seawater (personal desalting process).

* Food

■ *Supplies*

» You will need a three- to five-day supply of food for emergency situations and then think about more long-term plans for an end-times scenario.

» Off the grocery shelf (rotate with good dates).

□ Canned goods, including beans, chicken, turkey, tuna, salmon, soups and vegetables.

□ Freeze-dried fruits and vegetables.

□ Jerky.

□ Peanut butter, nuts and seeds.

□ Protein and/or energy bars.

» Pre-Packaged

□ Meals Ready-to-Eat (MRE) can be obtained online or at most outdoor sports stores. You will need to rotate MREs with the best dates.

□ Backpacking freeze-dried foods. These can be obtained online or at most outdoor sports stores.

□ Homegrown gardens/fruit trees. A great place for vegetables, spices and fruits.

□ Hunting. This is a bit trickier and more technical. It presupposes that you have access to hunting/trapping equipment and an area in which to hunt. Small game such as squirrel, birds, raccoon, possum and turkey can be trapped or hunted. Bigger game such as deer, elk and moose normally take a more experienced hunter.

□ Fishing. If you have access to an uncontaminated pond, creek, pond, stream or lake, you can take advantage of fishing for your food.

* Equipment/Procedures

■ *Survival Needs.*

» Certain items are required in an emergency. FEMA recommends the following:

□ A Bible.

□ Prescription medications, at least a week's worth.

□ Don't forget non-prescription medications.

- ☐ Cash in case ATMs are unavailable or credit/debit card systems are down.
- ☐ Important documents. Keep copies of any documents you cannot lose, along with your family emergency plan.
- ☐ Kitchen items.
- ☐ Manual can opener.
- ☐ Utensils, cups, Tupperware, napkins, plastic ties, garbage bags and disinfectant wipes.
- ☐ Personal hygiene items such as moist towelettes and hand sanitizer. Also, don't forget toothbrushes and toothpaste.
- ☐ Blanket and clothes. Keep a spare set of clothes and blankets to keep warm and dry.
- ☐ A battery-powered or hand-cranked radio, preferably a NOAA weather radio, for when there are no more batteries.
- ☐ Flashlights and extra batteries.
- ☐ Light sticks (glow sticks).
- ☐ First-aid kit and dust masks for any medical needs and to help filter contaminated air.
- ☐ Whistle and local map. You can use the whistle to signal for help and evacuate without GPS if needed.
- ☐ Cell phone and charger. Include a solar charger and/or fully charged power banks (will need to be recharged).
- ☐ Plastic sheeting and duct tape to help shelter in place, if needed.
- ☐ Consider a nylon rope.
- ☐ Wrench or pliers to turn off utilities.
- ☐ A multipurpose, multifunctional tool.
- ☐ Hand-warmers.
- ☐ Waterproof matches.
- ☐ Gloves.
- ☐ Pocket knife.
- ☐ Fire extinguisher.

## ★ Additional Items

- ■ *In addition to the above, here are some things we recommend you have or at least think about.*
  - » Non-digital or Lensatic compass when there is no GPS available.
  - » Firearms (depending on where you live) for self-protection and hunting. The best firearm for emergencies is what we call a takedown .22 caliber rifle, designed to be taken apart, which fits into your backpack. Having a shotgun and/or handgun is

ideal as well. Plenty of ammo in each caliber you are using.

» Bow/arrows. Compound or recurve.

» Solar-powered generator. When there is no fuel available, this gem will come in handy.

» Self-powered or hand-cranked flashlights for when there are no more batteries.

» Parachute cord (550). This comes in different lengths. We recommend as much as possible, four hundred yards or more.

» Survival knife.

» Cold weather boots, pants and jackets.

» Cold weather tent, sleeping bags and tarps.

» Multi-tool shovel.

» Fishing equipment and bait and hooks.

» Saw.

» Bolt cutter.

* Training

■ *It does no good to have the equipment listed above if you are not prepared and trained to use it. Get smart, especially with firearm safety, about all things listed.*

» Get trained or take courses in emergency preparedness. Many unexpected things can and do happen, so be prepared for those eventualities.

» Train with other professionals and/or believers. We survive better in groups when others have expertise in areas we do not.

# NOTES

## Chapter 1: The Making of a Warrior

1. Adam Nagourney, David E. Sanger, and Johanna Barr, "Hawaii Panics After Alert About Incoming Missile Is Sent in Error," *New York Times*, January 13, 2018, https://www.nytimes.com/2018/01/13/us/hawaii-missile.html.

2. Chris Hedges, "What Every Person Should Know About War," *New York Times*, July 6, 2003, https://www.nytimes.com/2003/07/06/books/chapters/what-every-person-should-know-about-war.html.

3. Religion News Service, "Shock Poll: Startling Numbers of Americans Believe World Now in the 'End Times,'" RNS Press Release Archive, September 11, 2013, https://religionnews.com/2013/09/11/shock-poll-startling-numbers-of-americans-believe-world-now-in-the-end-times.

4. Aaron Earls, "Vast Majority of Pastors See Signs of End Times in Current Events," *LifeWay Research*, April 7, 2020, https://lifewayresearch.com/2020/04/07/vast-majority-of-pastors-see-signs-of-end-times-in-current-events.

5. *Britannica*, s.v. "Balfour Declaration," by the Editors of *Encyclopaedia Britannica*, accessed June 19, 2020, https://www.britannica.com/event/Balfour-Declaration; see also History.com Editors, "Balfour Declaration," *History*, August 21, 2018, https://www.history.com/topics/middle-east/balfour-declaration.

6. *Britannica*, s.v. "Israel," by Russell A. Stone, Harvey Sicherman, William L. Ochsenwald, Eliahu Elath, accessed June 19, 2020, https://www.britannica.com/place/Israel; see also History.com Editors, "State of Israel Proclaimed," *History*, May 12, 2020, https://www.history.com/this-day-in-history/state-of-israel-proclaimed.

7. Ker Than, "Scientists: Natural Disasters Becoming More Common," *Live Science*, October 17, 2005, https://www.livescience.com/414 -scientists-natural-disasters-common.html; see also Farshid Vahedifard and Amir Aghakouchak, "The Risk of 'Cascading' Natural Disasters Is on the Rise," *Phys.org*, October 22, 2018, https://phys.org/news/2018-10 -cascading-natural-disasters.html.

8. Deborah Lee James and Mark A. Welsh III, "United States RPA Vector: Vision and Enabling Concepts 2013–2038," United States Air Force, February 17, 2014, https://www.af.mil/Portals/1/documents/news /USAFRPAVectorVisionandEnablingConcepts2013–2038.pdf.

9. Zachary Evans, "Kissinger Warns U.S. and China in 'Foothills of a Cold War,'" *National Review*, November 21, 2019, https://www.nationalreview .com/news/kissinger-warns-u-s-and-china-in-foothills-of-a-cold-war.

10. Joel C. Rosenberg, "What Does the Bible Teach about Pestilence, Plagues & Global Pandemics?," *Joel C. Rosenberg's Blog*, March 28, 2020, https://flashtrafficblog.allisrael.com/2020/03/28/what-does-the-bible -teach-about-pestilence-plagues-global-pandemics-so-many-are-asking -that-the-joshua-fund-and-i-have-published-a-fact-sheet-for-pastors -ministry-leaders-lay-people-and-the-medi.

## Chapter 2: Battle Ready!

1. Lt. Gen. Ken Dahl, November 29, 2018, telephone interview with Troy Anderson.

2. Anastasia Clark and Chris Bell, "Smartphone Users Warned to Be Careful of the Antichrist," *BBC News*, January 8, 2019, https://www .bbc.com/news/blogs-trending-46794556.

3. Glenn Greenwald, "XKeyscore," *The Guardian*, July 31, 2013, https:// www.theguardian.com/world/2013/jul/31/nsa-top-secret-program -online-data; see also Joseph Candel, "The Antichrist and Technology," Countdown to Armageddon, May 2015, https://countdown.org/en/entries /features/the-antichrist-and-technology.

4. *Holocaust Encyclopedia*, s.v. "Documenting Numbers: Victims of the Holocaust and Nazi Persecution," by the United States Holocaust Memorial Museum, accessed June 19, 2020, https://encyclopedia.ushmm .org/content/en/article/documenting-numbers-of-victims-of-the-holo caust-and-nazi-persecution.

5. Cristina Maza, "Christian Persecution and Genocide Is Worse Now Than 'Any Time in History,' Report Says," *Newsweek*, January 4, 2018, https:// www.newsweek.com/christian-persecution-genocide-worse-ever-770462.

6. Lindy Lowry, "Christian Persecution by the Numbers," *Open Doors*, January 16, 2019, https://www.opendoorsusa.org/christian-persecution /stories/christian-persecution-by-the-numbers.

7. Philippe Bohström, "Exclusive: Royal Burial in Ancient Canaan May Shed New Light on Biblical City," *National Geographic*, March 13, 2018, https://www.nationalgeographic.com/news/2018/03/megiddo -armageddon-dna-royal-burial-canaan-archaeology; see also Christina Lin, "Israel's Oil in Golan, Megiddo-Jezreel Valley," *The Times of Israel*, November 20, 2015, https://blogs.timesofisrael.com/israels-oil-in-golan -megiddo-jezreel-valley.

8. Joel Richardson, November 5, 2018, telephone interview with Troy Anderson.

9. Lt. Col. Scott Koeman, November 10, 2018, telephone interview with Troy Anderson.

10. Admiral J. J. Clark, "Top Five Priorities: Future Readiness," United States Navy, July 21, 2000, https://www.navy.mil/navydata/cno/cno-top 5futready.html.

## Chapter 3: Knowing Your Enemy

1. Liz Frazier, "S2 Army Officer Duties," *Career Trend*, December 28, 2018, https://careertrend.com/list-6692783-s2–army-officer-duties .html.

2. Capt. Norman H. Fuss III, "Back to the Basics: The Battalion S2," *Military Intelligence Professional Bulletin*, April-June 1997, https://fas .org/irp/agency/army/mipb/1997–2/fuss.htm.

3. Eric Jackson, "Sun Tzu's 31 Best Pieces of Leadership Advice," *Forbes*, May 23, 2014, https://www.forbes.com/sites/ericjackson/2014/05 /23/sun-tzus-33–best-pieces-of-leadership-advice/#34e4570f5e5e.

4. Dr. Robert Jeffress, June 27, 2019, telephone interview with Troy Anderson.

5. Ibid.

6. *Bible Study Tools*, s.v. "Arche," by Thayer and Smith, accessed June 19, 2020, https://www.biblestudytools.com/lexicons/greek/nas/arche .html.

7. Whitney Hopler, "Archangels: God's Leading Angels," *Learn Religions*, May 1, 2019, https://www.learnreligions.com/archangels-gods -leading-angels-123898.

8. Lela Gilbert, "Iran's Aggression and the Shi'ite Apocalypse," *Jerusalem Post*, August 17, 2019, https://www.jpost.com/opinion/irans-aggression -and-the-shiite-apocalypse-598904; see also Adam Eliyahu Berkowitz, "Battle of the Messiahs: Iran Hastening Process of Mahdi's Arrival with Horrific Chaos Around the World," *Breaking Israel News*, September 3, 2015, https://www.breakingisraelnews.com/48214/nuclear-deal-irans -attempt-create-horrific-chaos-prophesied-before-final-coming-islamic -messiah-middle-east.

9. Aaron Bandler, "Turkish President Says He Opposes All Allies of Israel," *Jewish Journal*, August 1, 2019, https://jewishjournal.com/news /israel/302438/turkish-president-says-he-opposes-all-allies-of-israel.

10. Joel Richardson, November 5, 2018, telephone interview with Troy Anderson.

11. Maj. Gen. Robert F. Dees, May 30, 2019, telephone interview with Troy Anderson.

12. Msgr. Charles Pope, "What Does the Bible Mean by 'the Flesh'?" *Community in Mission* (blog), Archdiocese of Washington, March 17, 2011, http://blog.adw.org/2011/03/what-does-the-bible-mean-by-the-flesh.

## Chapter 4: Center of Gravity

1. Dale C. Eikmeier, "The Center of Gravity: Still Relevant After All These Years?" *Military Review*, May 11, 2017, https://www.armyupre ss.army.mil/Journals/Military-Review/Online-Exclusive/2017–Online -Exclusive-Articles/The-Center-of-Gravity.

2. Mark P. Krieger Jr., "We the People Are Not the Center of Gravity in an Insurgency," *Military Review*, July-August 2007, https://www.questia .com/library/journal/1G1–166432652/we-the-people-are-not-the-center -of-gravity-in-an.

3. Mandy Katz, "Do We Divide the Holiest Holy City?" *Moment*, May 8, 2012, https://momentmag.com/do-we-divide-the-holiest-holy -city.

4. Maj. Gen. Robert F. Dees, May 30, 2019, telephone interview with Troy Anderson.

5. Ibid.

6. Aaron Earls, "Vast Majority of Pastors See Signs of End Times in Current Events," *LifeWay Research*, April 7, 2020, https://lifewayre search.com/2020/04/07/vast-majority-of-pastors-see-signs-of-end-times -in-current-events.

7. Ibid.

8. Daniel J. Smith, Kelley Jeter, and Odin Westgaard, "Three Approaches to Center of Gravity Analysis: The Islamic State of Iraq and the Levant," *Joint Force Quarterly*, 78, July 1, 2015, https://ndupress.ndu .edu/Media/News/Article/607722/three-approaches-to-center-of-gravity -analysis-the-islamic-state-of-iraq-and-th.

## Chapter 5: Fog of War

1. Maxwell P. Thurman, "Strategic Leadership," presentation to the Strategic Leadership Conference, U.S. Army War College, Carlisle Barracks, Pennsylvania, February 11, 1991.

2. Samuel Popejoy, "10 Alleged Secret Weapons of the US Military," *ListVerse*, January 30, 2018, https://listverse.com/2018/01/30/10–alleged -secret-weapons-of-the-us-military.

3. Ibid.

4. Chad Storlie, "Managing and Leading in the Midst of Uncertainty: Lessons from the Military," *Oxford Leadership*, 2015, https://www .oxfordleadership.com/wp-content/uploads/2016/08/oxford-leadership -managing-in-the-midst-of-uncertainty.pdf.

## Chapter 6: Vision

1. Sun Tzu, "The Art of War," trans. Lionel Giles, *The Internet Classics Archive*, 2009, http://classics.mit.edu/Tzu/artwar.html.

2. Department of the Army, "Army Doctrine Publication, No. 1," section 3-5, United States Army, July 31, 2019, https://armypubs.army.mil/epubs /DR_pubs/DR_a/pdf/web/ARN18008_ADP-1%20FINAL%20WEB.pdf.

3. From the foreword by David G. Perkins in *Multi-Domain Battle: Evolution of Combined Arms for the 21st Century* (2025–2040), United States Army, December 2017, https://www.tradoc.army.mil/Portals/14 /Documents/MDB_Evolutionfor21st%20(1).pdf.

4. Dr. Robert Jeffress, June 27, 2019, telephone interview with Troy Anderson.

5. Rabbi Berel Wein, "The Weimar Republic, Hyperinflation, and How They Paved the Way for Hitler," *Jewish History* (blog), *JewishHistory.org*, March 5, 2010, https://www.jewishhistory.org/weimar-republic.

6. Joel Richardson, November 5, 2018, telephone interview with Troy Anderson.

7. Loren Savini, "Human Microchipping Is Here, and It's About to Rock Your Skin's World," *Allure*, March 26, 2018, https://www.allure .com/story/rfdi-microchip-implant-in-ski.

8. Catherine Stupp, "The Humble Office Badge Is About to Be Unrecognizable," *Wall Street Journal*, January 6, 2020, https://www.wsj.com /articles/the-humble-office-id-badge-is-about-to-be-unrecognizable-11 578333651.

9. Arthur W. Pink, *The Antichrist Revised* (Ingersoll, Ontario, Canada: Devoted Publishing, 2019), 26.

## Chapter 7: Courage

1. United States Army, "Living the Army Values: Seven Core Army Values," *Lifestyles*, October 8, 2018, https://www.goarmy.com/soldier -life/being-a-soldier/living-the-army-values.html.

2. Col. Peter Brzezinski, October 12, 2018, telephone interview with Troy Anderson.

3. Telegraph Reporters, "Preacher Locked Up for Hate Crime after Quoting the Bible to Gay Teenager," *The Telegraph*, February 5, 2017, https://www.telegraph.co.uk/news/2017/02/05/preacher-locked-hate-crime-quoting-bible-gay-teenager; see also Ben Schreckinger, "Has a Civil Rights Stalwart Lost Its Way?" *Politico*, July/August 2017, https://www.politico.com/magazine/story/2017/06/28/morris-dees-splc-trump-southern-poverty-law-center-215312.

4. *Britannica*, s.v. "Constantine I," by J.F. Matthews, Donald MacGillivray Nicol, May 18, 2020, https://www.britannica.com/biography/Constantine-I-Roman-emperor.

5. Lindy Lowry, "Christian Persecution by the Numbers," *Open Doors*, January 16, 2019, https://www.opendoorsusa.org/christian-persecution/stories/christian-persecution-by-the-numbers.

6. Frank J. Gaffney, March 26, 2019, interview by Troy Anderson; see also "Modern Persecution," *Christianity.com*, May 3, 2010, https://www.christianity.com/church/church-history/timeline/1901–2000/modern-persecution-11630665.html.

7. Maj. Gen. Robert F. Dees, May 30, 2019, telephone interview with Troy Anderson.

8. S.L.A. Marshall, *Men Against Fire: The Problem of Battle Command* (Norman, Okla.: University of Oklahoma Press, 1947), 4, https://books.google.com/books?id=rzLxoITDhQQC&printsec=frontcover#v=onepage&q&f=false.

## Chapter 8: Checklists

1. Atul Gawande, *The Checklist Manifesto*, (New York: Metropolitan Books, 2009), quoted in Sam Thomas Davies, "The Checklist Manifesto by Atul Gawande" *Samuelthomasdavies.com*, https://www.samuelthomasdavies.com/book-summaries/health-fitness/the-checklist-manifesto.

2. Department of the Army, "Introduction to Pre-Combat Checks and Inspections," United States Army (AskTOP.net), http://asktop.net/wp/download/31/MSL_201_L11a_Intro_to_Pre-Combat_Checks_and_Inspections.pdf.

3. "What the B-17 Taught Us About Checklists," 2013, Angle of Attack, https://www.flyaoamedia.com/aoa/what-the-b17–taught-us-about-checklists/.

4. Ibid.

5. Brian Niemietz, "Hulk Hogan: Jesus, Not a Coronavirus Vaccine, Is What We Need," *New York Daily News*, April 7, 2020, https://www.nydailynews.com/snyde/ny-hulk-hogan-no-vaccine-find-jesus-coronavirus-20200407–dzc4615gv5cexpg57wdkvjyqma-story.html?fbclid=IwAR2cq6G0Zoy4s8CjPDaPJ8ck_VJvZAcDATKuTi7BbFC14El4OozrtSSSS_I.

6. Sid Roth, June 24, 2019, telephone interview with Troy Anderson.

## Chapter 9: Boot Camp

1. Col. Peter Brzezinski, October 12, 2018, telephone interview with Troy Anderson.

2. Lt. Col. Scott Koeman, October 10, 2018, telephone interview with Troy Anderson.

3. Joel Richardson, November 5, 2018, telephone interview with Troy Anderson.

4. Adm. William H. McRaven, "Admiral McRaven's Urges Graduates to Find Courage to Change the World," *UT News*, University of Texas at Austin, May 16, 2014, https://news.utexas.edu/2014/05/16/mcraven" -urges-graduates-to-find-courage-to-change-the-world/.

5. Department of the Army, "Battle Focused Training," United States Army, September 15, 2003, https://www.globalsecurity.org/military/library /policy/army/fm/7–1/fm7–1.pdf.

## Chapter 10: Spartan Warrior Training

1. Maj. Gen. Robert F. Dees, May 30, 2019, telephone interview with Troy Anderson.

2. Col. Peter Brzezinski, October 12, 2018, telephone interview with Troy Anderson.

3. Ginger Zee and Ella Torres, "More Than 1 Billion Animals Estimated Dead in Australia Wildfires: Expert," *ABC News*, January 8, 2020, https:// abcnews.go.com/International/billion-animals-estimated-dead-australia -wildfires/story?id=68143966; National Interagency Fire Center, "National Year-to-Date Report on Fires and Acres Burned," June 15, 2020, https://gacc .nifc.gov/sacc/predictive/intelligence/NationalYTDbyStateandAgency.pdf.

4. Dwayne Brown and JoAnna Wendel, "Scientists Planning Now for Asteroid Flyby a Decade Away," *NASA Jet Propulsion Laboratory*, California Institute of Technology, April 29, 2019, https://www.jpl.nasa.gov /news/news.php?feature=7390.

5. Sebastian Kettley, "Asteroid Warning: NASA Reveals 10 Dates 'God of Chaos' Asteroid Apophis Could Hit Earth," *Express*, November 22, 2019, https://www.express.co.uk/news/science/1206253/Asteroid-Apophis-news -NASA-tracker-dates-God-of-Chaos-asteroid-hit-Earth-NASA-warning.

6. Alan Rappeport and Jeanna Smialek, "I.M.F. Predicts Worst Downturn Since the Great Depression," *New York Times*, April 14, 2020, https:// www.nytimes.com/2020/04/14/us/politics/coronavirus-economy-recess ion-depression.htm

7. Klaus Schwab, "Now Is the Time for a 'Great Reset,'" *World Economic Forum*, June 3, 2020, https://www.weforum.org/agenda/2020/06 /now-is-the-time-for-a-great-reset.

8. Brett and Kate McKay, "The Spartan Way: The Mindset and Tactics of a Battle-Ready Warrior," *A Man's Life: Ancient Greece*, March 13, 2020, https://www.artofmanliness.com/articles/the-spartan-way-the-mindset-and-tactics-of-a-battle-ready-warrior. Used by permission.

9. Ibid.

10. Ethan Siegel, "This Is How We Know There Are Two Trillion Galaxies in the Universe," *Forbes*, October 18, 2018, https://www.forbes.com/sites/startswithabang/2018/10/18/this-is-how-we-know-there-are-two-trillion-galaxies-in-the-universe/#5d4f29e85a67.

## Chapter 11: Rest and Recuperation

1. Lisa Cannon Green, "Despite Stresses, Few Pastors Give Up on Ministry," *LifeWay Research*, September 1, 2015, https://lifewayresearch.com/2015/09/01/despite-stresses-few-pastors-give-up-on-ministry.

2. See *Britannica*, s.v. "Adullam," by the Editors of *Encyclopaedia Britannica*, accessed, June 22, 2020, https://www.britannica.com/place/Adullam-ancient-city-Israel.

3. Joel Richardson, November 5, 2018, telephone interview with Troy Anderson.

4. Dr. Robert Mawire, February 6, 2020, telephone interview with Troy Anderson.

5. John Ramirez, August 23, 2019, interview with Troy Anderson.

6. KP, "A Screwtape Letter for the Media Age," *The Christian Mind* (blog), November 22, 2005, http://christianmind.blogspot.com/2005/11/screwtape-letter-for-media-age.html.

## Chapter 12: Obstacles, Obstructions and Opportunities

1. "Afghanistan," September 2019, United Nations Mine Action Service, https://unmas.org/en/programmes/Afghanistan.

2. John Ramirez, August 23, 2019, interview with Troy Anderson.

3. Dr. Robert Mawire, February 6, 2020, telephone interview with Troy Anderson.

4. Dr. Tim LaHaye and Ed Hindson, *The Popular Encyclopedia of Bible Prophecy* (Eugene, Ore.: Harvest House, 2004), 23–27.

5. Vice Admiral Kevin D. Scott, "Joint Publication 3–15: Barriers, Obstacles, and Mine Warfare for Joint Operations," United States Department of Defense, September 6, 2016, https://www.jcs.mil/Portals/36/Documents/Doctrine/pubs/jp3_15pa.pdf?ver=2018–03–14–173117–737.

## Chapter 13: Weapons and Firepower

1. Lt. Gen. Ken Dahl, November 29, 2018, telephone interview with Troy Anderson.

2. John Ramirez, August 23, 2019, interview with Troy Anderson.

3. "MK 15—Phalanx Close-In Weapons System (CIWS)," accessed June 22, 2020, America's Navy, https://www.public.navy.mil/surfor/Pages/Phalanx-CIWS.aspx.

4. Mimi Elliott, "Christy Wimber: Naturally Supernatural," *CBN.com*, https://www1.cbn.com/700club/christy-wimber-naturally-super natural.

## Chapter 14: Prepping for the End Times

1. Carl von Clausewitz, *Vom Kriege*, trans. J.J. Graham, 1873, https://www.clausewitz.com/readings/OnWar1873/BK1ch03.html#a; see also U.S. Marine Corps Lieutenant General John E. Wissler, Heritage.org, "Logistics: The Lifeblood of Military Power," October 4, 2018, https://www.heritage.org/military-strength-topical-essays/2019-essays/logistics-the-lifeblood-military-power.

2. "Build a Kit," April 27, 2020, U.S. Department of Homeland Security, https://www.ready.gov/kit.

3. Lt . Gen. Ken Dahl, November 29, 2018, telephone interview with Troy Anderson.

4. For a more in-depth and detailed explanation, see *Studylight.org*, s.v. "Bible Commentaries: Expository Notes of Dr. Thomas Constable, Matthew 25," accessed June 25, 2020, https://www.studylight.org/comm entaries/dcc/matthew-25.html; see also Dr. John F. Walvoord, "Chapter 25: Judgments at the End of the Age," in *Matthew: Thy Kingdom Come*, https://walvoord.com/article/219.

5. Joel Richardson, November 5, 2018, telephone interview with Troy Anderson.

6. Joel Richardson, November 5, 2018, telephone interview with Troy Anderson.

7. Mark Solseth and Col. Brent Coryell, "A CRISIS Exists: An Easy Mnemonic to Remember the Sustainment Principles," April 23, 2018, https://www.army.mil/article/200199/a_crisis_exists_an_easy_mnemonic_to_remember_the_sustainment_principles; see also Maj. Gen. Rodney D. Fogg, "ADP 4–0: Sustainment," United States Army, July 2019, https://armypubs.army.mil/epubs/DR_pubs/DR_a/pdf/web/ARN18450_ADP%204-0%20FINAL%20WEB.pdf.

## Chapter 15: Coming Home

1. Rick Warren, "Next Time Will Be Different!" (sermon), Saddleback Church, December 23, 2019, https://saddleback.com/watch/come-and-see/next-time-will-be-different?autoplay=true.

2. Ibid.

3. Jonathan Bernis, March 12, 2020, telephone interview with Troy Anderson.

4. Ibid.

5. Nathan Tabor, *The Beast on the East River: The U. N. Threat to America's Sovereignty and Security* (Nashville: Nelson, 2006), 208.

6. Jonathan Bernis, March 12, 2020, telephone interview with Troy Anderson.

7. Ed Yong, "COVID-19 Can Last for Several Months," *Atlantic*, June 4, 2020, https://www.theatlantic.com/health/archive/2020/06/covid-19 –coronavirus-longterm-symptoms-months/612679/.

End-times expert, scholar, author, writer, speaker and owner of the Warrior Refuge, a 46-acre ministry resort near Columbus, Georgia, **U.S. Army Chaplain (Colonel) David J. Giammona** retired in June 2018 after 32 years of military service in the Army. His last assignment was the Installation Management Command (IMCOM) in San Antonio, Texas, where he was responsible for religious support on all 75 Army installations worldwide. He had oversight and administrative responsibility for more than 1,000 chaplains, religious affairs specialists, civilians and others, along with several thousand volunteers. Giammona was the strategic advisor to a three-star commanding general and the chief executor for the chief of chaplains to deliver world-class religious support services. Upon Giammona's retirement, President Donald Trump, U.S. Senator Ted Cruz, Pastor Rick Warren, *New York Times* bestselling author Max Lucado, actor Gary Sinise ("Lieutenant Dan" in *Forrest Gump*) and others sent him letters to express their appreciation for his service to his country.

An ordained Assemblies of God minister since 1988, Giammona has dedicated his life in retirement to writing and speaking with a focus on preparing the Church and the world for the end times.

His education includes an M.Div., Golden Gate Baptist Seminary; an M.S. in counseling—marriage/family therapy, Columbus State University; and an M.S.S. (master of strategic studies) at the U.S. Army War College.

His Army assignments include four years in the Pentagon as the Installation Management Command chaplain personnel assignments officer and the personnel assignments officer for the chief of chaplains; three tours of combat duty in Iraq, Afghanistan and Saudi Arabia; and extensive travel throughout the world as a trainer, mentor and coach to the military. Generals, fellow chaplains and colonels who served with Giammona describe him as "very highly revered," a "heavy hitter" with "gravitas," a "servant leader" who could "help lead through tough situations," and a chaplain and colonel chosen for this position because of his "compassion, his skills, and his love of God and country." "He was well liked and very well respected among people at IMCOM," says retired U.S. Army Major General Warren Patterson. "IMCOM was the headquarters of about 600 to 700 people, and he reached out to them. He had the utmost respect of everybody there. His staff absolutely loved him because he cared about them."

His awards and decorations include the Legion of Merit, Bronze Star Medal, Meritorious Service Medal, Joint Service Commendation Medal, Global War on Terror Service Medal, and Global War on Terrorism Expeditionary Medal.

Giammona is a native of Sacramento, California. He and his wife, Esther, have been married since October 1979 and have three adult children: Micah, Catarina and Melissa. Each is married and serving Christ. Giammona and Esther also have four grandchildren: Isaac, Michael, Eva and Faith. Colonel Giammona and Esther live at their home on the 46-acre Warrior Refuge ministry resort near Columbus, Georgia.

In his free time, the world-class motivational speaker enjoys playing the saxophone, working out, hunting and reading. He has an extensive background in music and graduated with a degree in saxophone performance from Sacramento State University. He speaks and performs at churches, conferences and other venues. Discover more at www.DavidJGiammona.com. Follow him on social media at Facebook.com/GiammonaDavid and Twitter.com/GiammonaDavid.

**Troy Anderson** is a Pulitzer Prize–nominated investigative journalist, bestselling co-author of *The Babylon Code* and *Trumpocalypse*, senior editor of *GODSPEED* magazine, former executive editor of *Charisma* magazine and Charisma Media, speaker and television and radio commentator. He spent two decades working as a reporter, bureau chief and editorial writer at the *Los Angeles Daily News, The Press-Enterprise* and other newspapers. He writes for Reuters, *Newsmax,* Townhall, *Christianity Today, Charisma, Human Events, Outreach* and other media outlets. He is also the founder and editor-in-chief of *Prophecy Investigators* (www.prophecyinvestigators.org), an online news and commentary magazine.

He appears regularly on GOD TV, *The Jim Bakker Show, Jewish Voice with Jonathan Bernis,* SkyWatchTV, Prophecy in the News, *Hagee Hotline,* Cornerstone TV Network's *Real Life* show, and many nationally syndicated radio shows.

He has interviewed many prominent national figures, including Billy Graham, Franklin Graham, Anne Graham Lotz, Pastor Rick Warren, Dr. Tim LaHaye, Hal Lindsey, Noam Chomsky, Dr. Ben Carson, David Horowitz, Patrick Buchanan, Dinesh D'Souza, Pastor Greg Laurie, Joel Rosenberg, Rabbi Jonathan Cahn, Sid Roth, Rabbi Jonathan Bernis, John Ramirez, Pastor Mark Hitchcock, Nick Vujicic, Lee Strobel, Pat Boone and Kirk Cameron.

During his career, Anderson has received numerous journalistic accolades: more than two dozen local, state and national writing awards; 2011 and 2012 Eddie Awards (*Folio:* magazine's prestigious journalism awards); two 2015 Charlie

Awards (Florida Magazine Association's top award); and a Pulitzer Prize nomination.

He is a member of the American Society of Journalists and Authors, the nation's premier association of writers of nonfiction who have met ASJA's exacting standards of professional achievement. He is also a member of the Association of Ghostwriters, Investigative Reporters & Editors and a graduate of the Act One and Movieguide screenwriting programs.

Anderson graduated from the University of Oregon in 1991 with a B.A. in news-editorial journalism and a minor in political science. He lives with his family in Irvine, California. Discover more at www.troyanderson.us, www.prophecy investigators.org, www.troyandersonwriter.com and www. godspeedmag.com. Follow him on social media at Facebook. com/troyandersonwriter and Twitter.com/TroyMAnderson.